WALKING IN THE ALGARVE

About the Authors

Nike and Jacint met many years ago on a long coach journey as they both travelled into the unknown to build a new life in a different country. It wasn't long before they became inseparable. Travelling quickly emerged as their favourite activity: they had their first walking holiday in Madeira in 2008 and now wherever they go they try to find the best trails.

Nike went to journalism school and Jacint is a keen photographer. They really enjoy walking in the mountains and would happily spend every day on the trails. When they first visited the Algarve they were mesmerised by the diverse scenery and dramatic coastline. Having collected the best routes, first in Cyprus and now in the Algarve, they want to share their passion for walking with others.

Other Cicerone guides by the authors

Walking in Cyprus

WALKING IN THE ALGARVE

33 WALKS IN THE SOUTH OF PORTUGAL INCLUDING SERRA DE MONCHIQUE AND COSTA VICENTINA

by Nike Werstroh and Jacint Mig

CICERONE

JUNIPER HOUSE, MURLEY MOSS,
OXENHOLME ROAD, KENDAL, CUMBRIA LA9 7RL
www.cicerone.co.uk

Second edition 2019
ISBN: 978 1 85284 994 8
This completely new guide replaces *Walking in the Algarve* (9781852844370) by Julie Statham.

Printed in China on behalf of Latitude Press Ltd
A catalogue record for this book is available from the British Library.

Route mapping by Lovell Johns www.lovelljohns.com
Contains OpenStreetMap.org data © OpenStreetMap contributors, CC-BY-SA. NASA relief data courtesy of ESRI
All photographs are by the authors unless otherwise stated.

Acknowledgements

A special thank you to Alison Currier who read most of the walks. A big thank you to Jonathan Williams for suggesting we explore the Algarve.

Updates to this Guide

While every effort is made by our authors to ensure the accuracy of guidebooks as they go to print, changes can occur during the lifetime of an edition. Any updates that we know of for this guide will be on the Cicerone website (www.cicerone.co.uk/994/updates), so please check before planning your trip. We also advise that you check information about such things as transport, accommodation and shops locally. Even rights of way can be altered over time.

The route maps in this guide are derived from publicly available data, databases and crowd-sourced data. As such they have not been through the detailed checking procedures that would generally be applied to a published map from an official mapping agency, although naturally we have reviewed them closely in the light of local knowledge as part of the preparation of this guide.

We are always grateful for information about any discrepancies between a guidebook and the facts on the ground, sent by email to updates@cicerone.co.uk or by post to Cicerone, Juniper House, Murley Moss, Oxenholme Road, Kendal, LA9 7RL.

Register your book: To sign up to receive free updates, special offers and GPX files where available, register your book at www.cicerone.co.uk.

Front cover: Cliffs near Cabo São Vicente (Walk 27)

CONTENTS

Symbols used on route maps

- route
- alternative route
- start point
- finish point
- start/finish point
- route direction
- glacier
- woodland
- urban areas
- regional border
- international border
- station/railway
- peak
- manned/unmanned refuge
- campsite
- building
- church/monastery/cross
- castle
- pass
- water feature
- viewpoint
- picnic area
- parking
- windmill

Relief
in metres

- 5000 and above
- 4800–5000
- 4600–4800
- 4400–4600
- 4200–4400
- 4000–4200
- 3800–4000
- 3600–3800
- 3400–3600
- 3200–3400
- 3000–3200
- 2800–3000
- 2600–2800
- 2400–2600
- 2200–2400
- 2000–2200
- 1800–2000
- 1600–1800
- 1400–1600
- 1200–1400
- 1000–1200
- 800–1000
- 600–800
- 400–600
- 200–400
- 0–200

GPX files for all routes can be downloaded free at www.cicerone.co.uk/994/GPX.

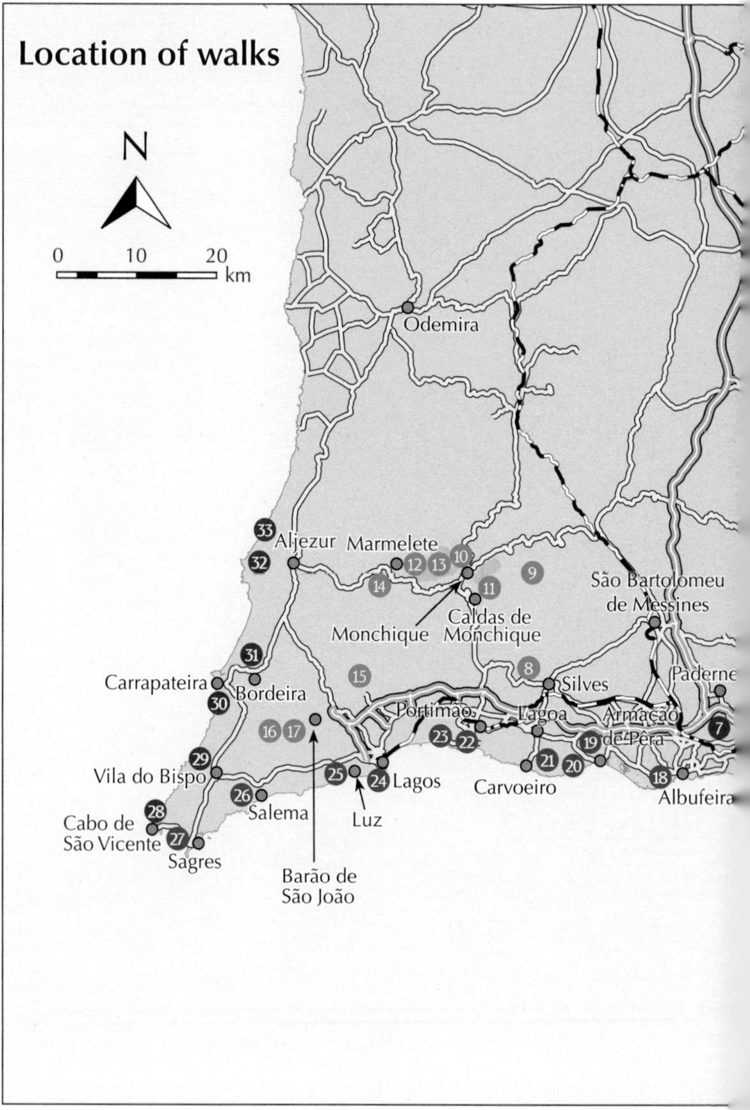
Location of walks
N
0
10
20
km
Odemira
Aljezur
Marmelete
Monchique
Caldas de Monchique
São Bartolomeu de Messines
Silves
Paderne
Carrapateira
Bordeira
Portimão
Lagoa
Armação de Pêra
Vila do Bispo
Lagos
Carvoeiro
Albufeira
Salema
Luz
Cabo de São Vicente
Sagres
Barão de São João
7
8
9
10
11
12
13
14
15
16
17
18
19
20
21
22
23
24
25
26
27
28
29
30
31
32
33

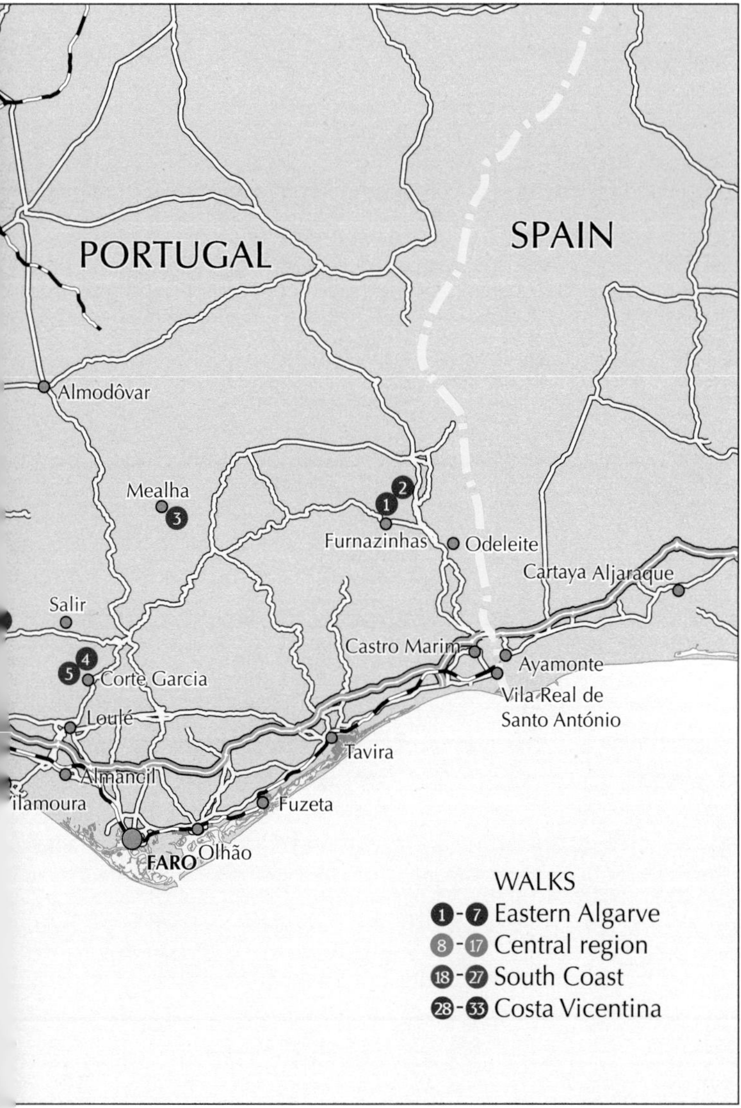
PORTUGAL
SPAIN
Almodôvar
Mealha
3
2
1
Furnazinhas
Odeleite
Cartaya Aljaraque
Salir
4
5
Corte Garcia
Castro Marim
Ayamonte
Vila Real de
Santo António
Loulé
Tavira
Almancil
ilamoura
Fuzeta
FARO
Olhão
WALKS
1-7 Eastern Algarve
8-17 Central region
18-27 South Coast
28-33 Costa Vicentina

Endless opportunities to enjoy the coastline near Praia do Barranco das Canas (Walk 22)

INTRODUCTION

Portugal's southernmost region, with its rugged coastline, hidden coves, rock-fringed sandy beaches and pleasant climate, has been attracting beach-loving tourists since the late 1960s. Small fishing villages have gradually grown into tourist resorts. Endless summer days see a great number of people in the coastal resorts. Admiring the sandy beaches surrounded by cliffs from the coastal path, it is not difficult to see why the sun-seekers come here.

For this reason, the Algarve is mostly known for its charming coast and inviting hot summers, but not too far from the busy beaches there are small, less-known villages where the way of life hasn't changed greatly over the past decades. Leaving the busy coast, carob and cork oak populate the hillsides, and almond and olive trees provide ingredients for local products.

Walking is the best way to explore the Algarve's surprisingly diverse scenery. The Algarve might not be considered a walking destination as there are no high mountains; however, there are two long-distance trails across the area. Shorter hiking and biking trails are advertised as well, and active holidays are encouraged for the growing number of people who want to explore beyond the sandy beaches.

Jagged coastlines washed with turquoise waters dominate the scenery in the south, and even in the early autumn, you can still stop for a swim on one of the remote sandy beaches. The narrow southern coastal path is easy to follow and it gives numerous opportunities to admire sinkholes and sea stacks created by the power of nature.

The waves of the Atlantic Ocean batter the Algarve's least-developed region, the wild western coast, constantly and without mercy, making the west coast beaches the must-visit playgrounds for experienced surfers.

Roaring wind greets you by the lighthouse of Cabo de São Vicente, and every part of the impressive coastline is moulded by the forceful elements. The outcrop with the lighthouse marked the end of the known world until the 14th century. But during the 15th century, Prince Henry the Navigator began the maritime expeditions from Lagos which helped to establish the Portuguese Empire and broaden the knowledge of the world.

Only about 30min drive from the coast, the Monchique Range – the highest part of the Algarve – is altogether different. Trails meander over the slopes near small, tranquil villages, surrounded by cork oak and eucalyptus. Locals work on their land and the meadows are often dotted with grazing animals.

Forest track descending from Cerro dos Negros (Walk 4)

By following the trails you can experience the many colours, sounds and smells of the Algarve through the seasons.

Almond flowers whiten the countryside like snow from late January. Spring arrives early, bringing fresh colours with its wide selection of orchids and wildflowers. In the summer, shimmering heat characterises the countryside and the scenery is parched. The ground is dry yellow and brown, and the dusty leaves hardly move in the gentle breeze. The golden sandy beaches are packed with holidaymakers and the coast is throbbing with life. Almonds and grapes are harvested in September, and late autumn brings some much-needed rain. During the short winter, streams come alive, happily gushing down over the rocks.

After a day spent walking in the countryside, on the coast or in the Monchique, you can enjoy a well-deserved seafood dinner in one of the coastal towns, or the popular Portuguese peri peri chicken in the small restaurants. And the fine local dishes should be accompanied with great local wine.

The Algarve was under Moorish rule for 500 years (AD 711–1250) and the name comes from this period, when it was called Al-Gharb (the west). Many town names and about 1000 words in the Portuguese language have an Arabic origin.

A stone building near Fonte Santa (Walk 9)

Many of the trails offer great views as well as interesting historical sights to look out for. You can still see some rusty *noras* (wells) in the countryside, ruins of forts and lighthouses along the coast, an abandoned hamlet on the slope of Fóia, or a megalithic burial site (built during the 3rd or 4th Millennium BC) near Mealha.

Many locals might think that walking for leisure is a strange activity, but they welcome the growing number of people who want to explore the diverse landscape on foot.

Deep sinkholes created by rain water and sea erosion

GEOGRAPHY AND GEOLOGY

The Algarve, the southernmost region of mainland Portugal, can be divided into three main regions: the *serra* (mountains), the *barrocal* (transition between the mountains and the coastal strip) and the coast.

Serra

The northern part of the Algarve, the Serra, forms part of the Iberian Massif. It consists of the shale terrain Monchique mountains and Caldeirão.

The Monchique Massif is a result of volcanic activity about 72 million years ago. This area consists of granite and schist. Today, pine trees, eucalyptus, cork oaks and shrubs grow on the slopes. The hills of Caldeirão consist of schist; cork oak and Mediterranean shrubs, such as rock roses, oaks, rosemary, and lavender populate the hillsides.

The barrocal

The Central Algarve, formed of clay and limestone is the transition between the 'mountains' and the coastal regions. The *barrocal* is formed of limestone from the Jurassic era. The hills and plains are today mainly characterised by agriculture. They are home to almond, orange, fig, carob, and olive trees. Mediterranean shrubs also grow in this area.

The coast

The rocky western coastline between Odeceixe and Vila do Bispo is carved into the Iberian Massif of dark-coloured shade and greywacke of the Paleozoic era, but the Pontal da Carrapateira area and the Sagres

Bigger sea stacks – such as these on Walk 22 can provide a safe nesting place for birds

Peninsula are made of the light-coloured limestone of the Mesozoic Era.

In Sagres and near Figueira beach, the limestone cliffs are Jurassic, while the most recent marl cliffs between Figueira and Porto de Mós are from the Cretaceous period. The cliffs between Porto de Mós and Olhos de Aqua are made of the younger carbonate rocks of the Miocene period. These rocks are sculpted by both fresh and sea water, creating a stunning coastal landscape with sea stacks, natural arches and coves.

CAVES, ARCHES, SEA STACKS, AND RUGGED COASTLINE

Waves slowly make their way into the cracks in the limestone rocks, gradually making a cave. The water-formed cave becomes larger over time, and when it breaks through, it creates an arch. It then gradually grows and when the top can no longer be supported, it collapses, leaving a stack behind.

The limestone of the Algarve coast is constantly changing form through a combination of erosion by the sea and rain water dissolving the calcium carbonate from the limestone, deepening the cracks in the rocks and creating sinkholes and caves. This type of activity can be observed along the coast of the Algarve.

*Sawfly Orchid (*Ophrys Tenthredinifera*); Naked Man Orchid (*Orchis italica*); Green-winged orchid (*Orchis morio picta*); Snapdragon (*Antirrhinum majus cirrhigerum*)*

PLANTS AND FLOWERS

In the springtime, wildflowers carpet the meadows and hillsides. White and pink rock roses flower and delicate orchids hide in the lush forests or grow on clifftops.

Orchids

There are numerous orchid species in the Algarve, and some of them appear as early as late January or early February. Many bloom during March and April and there are some that can still be seen in May and June. The best time to spot orchids – albeit with slight variation from year to year – is probably March and April. There is not room here to list all the species, but among the orchids you can spot during spring walks are the Bee orchid, one of the first to flower in the year; the Green-Winged orchid, which can be seen in April and May, and the Pyramidal orchid, which blooms in April and May in meadows and on clifftops.

The Naked Man orchid (*Orchis Italica*) flowers in April and May; you can see many along tracks and near the coast (for example Walk 25, Luz to Salema). You can also spot Sawfly Orchid (*Ophrys Tenthredinifera*) in March in Barão de São João Forest (Walk 16 and 17).

Carob

The carob tree (*Ceratonia siliqua*) is typical to the Mediterranean. It grows wild but is widely cultivated for its edible pods. The world 'carat' – the unit used to measure the purity of gold – is derived from the Greek word *keration*. The pods' small beans are of uniform size and were used to measure gold.

Carob is used in local products such as fig and carob cake, and a typical sweet and strong liqueur. Carob syrup is widely made and used, and carob powder is used to replace cocoa powder.

Cork oak

Portugal's biggest export product is cork, providing 50% of the world's supply. The cork oak can live up to 250 years and the bark can be harvested every nine years. There is a saying in Portugal: 'Plant a cork oak for your grandchildren', as the first harvest can only take place 25–30 years after the tree was planted. The bark is carefully cut by hand without cutting the tree down. The first two harvests

Cork oak (*Quercus suber*)

are usually made into granulates, used for sparkling wine stoppers. Only from the third harvest can the cork be used as a wine stopper.

While best known as a wine bottle stopper, cork has other uses. Purses, handbags and shoes are all made from cork and sold in the Algarve.

Almond trees

If you are walking between the end of January and March you will see almond trees in blossom. According to legend, when the Al-Gharb was ruled by the Moors, Prince Ibn-Almuncim fell in love and married Gilda, a Nordic princess. They lived in Silves, but in the winter, the princess missed the snow-covered landscape of her home country. Ibn-Almucim couldn't bear for his wife to be sad and ordered the planting of thousands of almond trees near the palace. When Gilda looked out of her window and saw the blossoming almond trees whitening the scenery like snow, her sadness was cured. Almond is used in many ways in Portugal; for cakes, sweets, marzipan, and even to make liqueurs.

WILDLIFE

A wide range of birds live in the Algarve, and due to its geographic location, many migrating birds spend part of the year there, making it a great place for birdwatching. Birdwatching walks are organised from many towns.

Storks build large distinctive nests on top of tall poles and chimneys. A stork nest on a house is believed to bring good luck and they are therefore protected. Storks are monogamous and they return to their nests year after year. The stork couple share parental duties and when the chicks grow to adulthood, they often build their nests close to the place where they grew up, so it is not unusual to see many nests close to each other in the same area. Near Silves, on the Levada Trail (Walk 8) it is possible to see flocks of storks searching for dinner. There are many nests on poles and trees near the road in Rasmalho, near Caldas de Monchique. The Costa Vicentina is the only place in Europe where the white storks nest on the coastal cliffs. You can spot stork nests on the cliffs near Arrifana, on the Fortaleza da Arrifana circular (Walk 32).

Small mammals such as rabbits, hare, hedgehogs, Egyptian mongoose, wild boar, red fox and bats inhabit the Algarve, but as most of them are nocturnal, you might not see any. Moorish gecko and fire salamander are also common, and most probably you will see frogs, lizards and butterflies.

The endangered Iberian lynx (*Lynx pardinus*) once populated the Iberian Peninsula. They feed mainly on rabbits and when the wild rabbit population declined dramatically during the second half of the 20th century, the lynx struggled to survive. By the 21st century it was on the verge of extinction. A breeding centre near Silves is part of the great effort to save the species. The centre protects animals from humans and doesn't allow visitors, as its aim is to release the animals into the wild. Several lynx have been successfully released since 2014.

Snakes

Eight species of snake can be found in the Algarve. Most of them are non-venomous; however the false smooth snake (*Macroprotodon cucullatus*) and the large Montpellier snake (*Malpolon monspessulanus*) are venomous. Fortunately, their fangs are placed too far back to really bite humans effectively. The Montpellier snake only attacks if handled, so don't disturb them.

The wary grass snake (*Natrix natrix*) is non-venomous but gets irritable if approached. The viperine snake (*Natrix maura*) can be found near water, is aggressive and strikes like a viper, but is non-venomous. Lataste's viper (*Vipera latastei*) is rare in the Algarve; it is about 70cm long, and grey with a dark zigzag pattern on its back. It is irritable and venomous, but not considered to be dangerous.

The horseshoe whip snake (*Hemorrhois hippocrepis*) can grow up to 1.5m, is common and can be aggressive but is non-venomous.

The non-venomous ladder snake (*Zamenis scalaris*) can grow up to 1.6m and is often found on rocks. The small southern smooth snake (*Coronella girondica*) is a chequered brownish colour and likes dry environments. It is non-venomous and usually active at dusk.

BRIFF HISTORY

There is evidence that humans inhabited the Algarve region as early as the Paleolithic and Neolithic periods. Megalithic stones found near Mealha village (Walk 3) are evidence of early human activity.

It is believed that pre-Celtic groups founded the city that is today known as Lagos, and around 1000BC the Phoenicians founded ports along the coast. It is believed that Portimão was founded in 550BC by the Carthaginians (it was called Portus Hanibalis at the time).

From around 218BC, the Algarve region was under Roman control, which continued for 600 years. From AD711, the Moors started to conquer the Iberian Peninsula, and in AD716 Lagos was occupied and named Zawaia. The Algarve was under Moorish rule for 500 years (711–1250) and during this time Silves became the capital of the region.

The Algarve's name comes from this period as it was called Al-Gharb ('the west') and there are about 1000 words in the Portuguese language, along with many town names, that have an Arabic origin. The Moors brought their irrigation systems and architecture with them. The typical chimneys in the Algarve also show a strong Arabic influence. The Moors introduced many plants to the area, for example fig trees, citrus, carob, almond and pomegranates.

There was a Catholic kingdom in the north of Portugal from the 8th

The waterwheel (nora) was introduced by the Arabs in the 8th century

century onwards, and it started to conquer the Moorish towns: by 1189, Silves was in Portuguese hands, and Moorish rule started to decline. By the middle of the 13th century, the Algarve region had become part of the Portuguese kingdom.

In the 15th century, Prince Henry the Navigator initiated the maritime expeditions from Lagos which helped to establish the Portuguese empire. During his time, Madeira, the Azores and the west coast of Africa were explored and the islands colonised. In 1434, Gil Eanes set sail from Lagos and sailed around Cape Bojador, west Africa. He was the first sailor to succeed in this and Lagos became an important trading port. The Portuguese then began to export slaves and gold from Africa. The fact that Lagos was the capital of the Algarve from 1577 shows the importance of the coastal town. During the 16th century Portuguese trade with Africa, Asia and Brazil boomed.

In 1578, in the battle of Alcácer Quibir in Morocco, Portugal lost its young king and a significant army and, as a subsequent result of these events, from 1580 Portugal was in dynastic union with Spain. Spanish kings ruled for 60 years. Portugal also lost its empire status in Asia. A rebellion against Spain began in 1640 and Portugal remained at war with Spain for the following 28 years. During this time, many fortifications were built along the Spanish-Portuguese border. Some of these fortresses can still be seen in the Algarve; for example in Alcoutim and in Castro Marim. From 1595 until the 19th century, the Algarve was a semi-autonomous region with its own tax system and governor.

In 1755, the Lisbon earthquake and the subsequent tsunami damaged many coastal towns, including Lagos and fortresses along the Algarve coast. Faro didn't suffer from the tsunami because the sandy banks of the Ria Formosa gave some protection, and therefore it became the Algarve's capital after the earthquake. During the 19th century and the first half of the 20th century, fishing and agriculture became the main activities in the Algarve.

Portugal joined the First World War to save its African colonies and to prevent a Spanish invasion. Germany

Forte de Almádena (Walk 25)

declared war on Portugal in March 1916. Portugal retained its colonies in Africa after the peace conference in Versailles in 1919, but – like many other countries – suffered from food shortages and inflation after the war. The political instability led to a military coup in 1926, and Portugal was then under dictatorship for almost 40 years. It remained neutral during WW2 and was an important escape route for many people from war-torn countries.

From the 1970s, tourists started to discover the Algarve region, and these days tourism is the mainstay of the Algarve's economy.

AZULEJOS

The distinctive ceramic tiles were brought to Portugal by the Moors in the 13th century, but were not widely used until the 16th and 17th centuries. *Azulejo* comes from an Arabic word meaning 'small polished stone'. The tiles were used to decorate the interiors of buildings and were originally decorated with geometric shapes. The Portuguese began to use them to tell historical and religious stories and they became a typical element of Portuguese architecture. The tiles have practical purposes as well as decorative. Interior tiles protected the building in hot weather, and help to keep rooms cool. The tiles are used for signs, and to decorate churches, stations and other public buildings, and can be seen in towns and villages throughout the country.

Mediterranean pine populate the hills near Barão de São João (Walk 16)

WHEN TO GO

You can enjoy most walks from September to June, but spring is perhaps the best time to discover the trails in the Algarve, when wildflowers give colour to the countryside and the temperature is warm but not too hot. Spring arrives early – in some years as early as January – with almond trees in bloom. From February there are orchids to look out for.

The summer months are generally too hot for walking, but in September you can still enjoy beach weather with fewer people, and stop for a swim along the coastal paths; however, make sure you take enough water and apply sun cream generously. If planning to walk in the winter, bear in mind that most rain occurs during the winter months, but the temperature is pleasant for walking. It can be a lot colder and windier on Fóia than on the south coast. The west coast is constantly battered by strong winds and can be colder than the rest of the Algarve.

GETTING THERE

The best way to get to the Algarve is to fly to Faro and then take local buses or hire a car to get around. As the Algarve is a popular destination, there are plenty of flights from the UK to Faro. EasyJet, Ryanair, Jet2, British Airways, TAP Air Portugal and TUI all offer flights from various UK airports. As always, shop around for the best deals.

GETTING AROUND

Car

Driving around with a hire car is an easy way to discover the Algarve. Many walking trails are easily accessible by car, and there are usually places to park at the beginning of the trail. If you are planning a linear walk, it might be a disadvantage to have a car parked at one end of the walk, but – especially on the coast – you can catch a bus or take a taxi back to your starting point. Also, most of the linear

Shrub-bordered sandy path on the west coast (Walk 32)

walks described in this book (except Walk 26) are not too long, giving you an opportunity to retrace your steps. However, if you opt to return to your start-point, always allow enough time and set off early. Walking on the coast usually takes a lot longer on the outward trip; you can probably retrace your steps in half the time if you don't revisit each outcrop on the way back.

You can hire a car at Faro airport or in most towns. You can find the well-known car hire companies and some local firms such as Centauro. You can get better deals by booking in advance online using price comparison websites. If you are planning to hire a car from the airport, it might be worth checking out companies based nearby. They have a shuttle bus service to take you to their offices and they can be cheaper than the well-known chains at the airport.

If you are planning to drive, bear in mind that the A22 is a toll road. You can rent a toll transponder with the car, however, make sure you know where and how to pay the fees before leaving the car hire office, as there are several troubling stories circulating online about the system and problems it can cause for tourists. If you don't want to worry about tolls, you can avoid the A22 toll road completely, instead using the N265 which runs almost parallel.

Buses

There is a fairly good bus service along the coast; however, it is difficult to get to some of the towns and villages. If you are planning to take buses to inland villages, then you will have to carefully check the timetable locally. If you are planning to get to and from the walks described in the book by bus, it is highly advisable to seek information at the local tourist office or bus terminal. Some of the popular and well-known beaches (for example Marinha and Benagil) are surprisingly difficult to reach without a car. At the end of most of the linear walks, it is possible to catch a bus back to the starting point along the coast. It is very important to check the bus timetable when making plans for Walk 26 (Salema to Sagres) as this is the longest coastal section, and retracing your steps might not be a realistic option. (However, accommodation can easily be found in coastal towns).

- http://eva-bus.com
- www.frotazul-algarve.pt
- www.algarvebus.info (unofficial but informative and up-to-date bus timetable)

Taxis

Taxis can be found in most of the towns mentioned in the book; however, if you are planning to use a taxi service to return to your starting point after completing a linear walk, it is advisable to make arrangements before setting off. Seek advice in local tourist offices.

Trains

Most of the villages mentioned in the book can't be reached by train. To check the trains between major towns, see www.cp.pt. You can also find information and timetables at the local tourist office and train station.

ACCOMMODATION

There are plenty of hotels and self-catering options in the coastal areas, and there are a range of options in the Monchique area; you can also find some accommodation in inland towns and villages. Make sure you book

Coastal path with great views near Praia do Paradíso (Walk 21)

through a trusted website. Airbnb features a wide selection of private rental apartments and houses both along the coast and inland (www.airbnb.co.uk). Details of campsites can be found at www.en.camping.info/portugal/algarve/campsites.

You may opt to tackle several day trips in the same area, or consider splitting your holiday between different bases. If you decide to stay in one place you can still enjoy different areas, as many locations are easily reached in a day trip.

WHAT TO TAKE

Pack what you would normally take for a day walk. Carry a waterproof jacket, as rain can arrive quickly. Take a warm fleece/jumper to the

Monchique range and to the west coast, especially during winter and spring.

Comfortable hiking boots, sun cream and a sun hat are essential; always carry ample water for your day. Don't forget your camera to capture the beautiful landscape.

There are no dedicated walking maps available for the Algarve. Walkers should be able to follow the routes described here without additional maps, however the Maps.me and/or ViewRanger applications provide local mapping should you need it.

WAYMARKING

The long-distance Via Algarviana, the GR13 (*Grand Rota*) is marked with red/white signs. The 300km trail, which starts at Alcoutim and finishes at Cabo de São Vincente, was completed in 2009 and aims to take walkers through the Algarve's diverse scenery.

The Rota Vicentina (including the Historical Way and Fishermen's Trail) along the west coast starts in Santiago do Cacém and finishes at the most south-westerly point in Europe, at Cabo de São Vicente. In Odeceixe the trail splits; the Fishermen's Trail stays closer to the coast while the Historical Trail runs slightly inland. There are also several short extension loops along the coast. Some sections of this western coastal path and some of the loops are used in this book. Green/blue waymarkers are used for the Rota Vicentina.

The authorities have recognised that, along with the beautiful beaches, active holidays are increasingly attracting tourists, and there are moves afoot to improve and promote the walking and cycling trails.

There is a plan in place to waymark the coastal path between Sagres and Luz as an extension of the existing Rota Vicentina long distance path.

Yellow/red signs are used on PR trails. Many of the trails are numbered. The routes are marked as PR (*pequena rota* – 'small route') followed by a number and the abbreviation which indicates the area/municipality. For example, the Marmelete circular (Walk 14) is marked as the PR6MCQ trail. At the beginning of the PR trail, there is usually an information board with a map and a short description of the walk and information about the area and local plants. Many marked trails use a cross (in the trail colours) to mark the wrong path at junctions. However, a few walks described in this book follow a path marked with a cross for a short section, such as Walk 7 Paderne Castle, Walk 9 Fonte Santa, Walk 17 Barão de São João Forest circular and Walk 29 Castelejo circular, but this is always mentioned in the description. Occasionally, a painted red spot can be seen on rocks on the western coastal path.

Please note that the signs indicating a left or right turn (especially in the Eastern Algarve) often appear well before the actual junction or turn off.

PR waymarking: wrong way; Simple directional signs; Rota Vicentina sign; Signed junction below the peak of Fóia; PR waymarking: right turn, correct route

USING THIS GUIDE

The walks in this guide are divided into four geographical sections. Each section begins with a brief introduction to the area and gives some information about potential bases from which to plan your walks.

An information box at the start of each walk provides the following information: start/finish point (including GPS co-ordinates), total distance, total ascent/descent, difficulty grade (see the grading information below), the length of time the walk is likely to take and details about refreshments and access that might be useful when planning your day. Snack bars and beach restaurants are mentioned when the trail arrives at or passes a beach, but bear in mind that many of these may only be open during the peak season (May to October).

Places and features that appear on the accompanying maps are shown in **bold** in the route description.

The times and distances given in the route information boxes and route summary table are from the start to the finish of the walk. Most of the coastal walks described in this book are linear, but it is possible to take a bus back or stay the night in the settlement where the walk finishes. However, always check the bus timetable locally, arrange a taxi or book accommodation in advance.

Views towards Praia do Burgau (Walk 25)

On most of the coastal routes, you can retrace your steps to return to your start-point (except on Walk 26 Salema to Sagres as this is 17km one-way on an undulating coastal path).

The grading in this guide is only an indicator: bad weather or poor visibility can make any walk more challenging. Strong winds on the west coast can make the coastal walks in that area more demanding.

- **Grade 1:** easy, and/or short walk, without any significant ascent/descent
- **Grade 2:** moderate, medium length or longer walk but mostly on easy terrain
- **Grade 3:** a longer walk and/or more difficult terrain

The times provided – both for the walks themselves and between landmarks/features – are approximate. The walk times do not take account of longer breaks for picnics or visiting attractions, or stopping at beaches. Once you have tried a few walks using this guide, you will be able to see how your own pace compares to the times given and adjust your planning accordingly.

The times given are fairly generous, especially on the coastal path, as you will need extra time if you follow the path closer to the cliffs and/or walk out onto the outcrops. It is possible that you might spend up to 4hr on a 10km trail (wandering out to outcrops, admiring the dramatic coast and hidden beaches) but if you want to retrace your steps – without visiting every outcrop or strictly following the closest path to the cliffs – you can do the same walk in about 2hr–2hr 30min on your return. This needs to be considered when planning a coastal walk.

Access to the trails is described in as much detail as possible. To help to identify the exact spot, GPS co-ordinates of the start-point are also given.

Where a waymarked trail is used, the trail number and the colours of the signage/waymarking are mentioned. Occasionally, the trail described takes an unmarked path or path with a cross, but this is always pointed out in the description.

The coastal path between Lagos and Cabo de São Vicente (Walks 24–27) can also be walked as a three or four-day trek, using accommodation in towns and villages along the trail. The other coastal walks (Walks 19–21) can be combined to extend the route to a full-day linear walk on the coast. Accommodation can be found in the coastal towns but in peak season it is best to book ahead.

GPX tracks

GPX tracks for the routes in this guidebook are available to download free at www.cicerone.co.uk/994/GPX. A GPS device is an excellent aid to navigation, but you should also carry a map and compass and know how to use them. GPX files are provided in good faith, but neither the author nor the publisher accept responsibility for their accuracy.

EASTERN ALGARVE

Narrow path towards Miradouro Norte (Walk 6)

EASTERN ALGARVE

A well and trough beside the trail (Walk 1)

Only a short distance from busy Faro and the popular beach resorts, there is a different Algarve with small villages such as **Furnazinhas** and **Mealha**, where the way of life hasn't changed greatly in decades. The hills and plains are mainly characterised by agriculture. Almond, orange, fig, carob and olive trees supply ingredients for local products. There is also evidence of early human activity in the area. There is a megalithic burial site (built during the 3rd or 4th millennium) near Mealha (Walk 3), and a defensive wall from the Iron Age near Penina. You can enjoy fine views of the hills from Rocha de Pena (Walk 6) and admire the remaining walls of Paderne Castle (Walk 7), which was originally built as a Moorish fort. It is believed to be one of the seven castles on the Portuguese flag, representing those taken by the Portuguese from the Moors. The walks in this area described here are all under 10km and not demanding.

Accommodation can be found in or near **Faro** as well as **Loulé** and in some of the small villages. Faro has everything the traveller might need; hotels and apartments, bars, restaurants and shops. The old town, encircled by ancient city walls, and the harbour are great for an afternoon stroll, and there are plenty of restaurants and cafés where you can sample the local food. There are some small but busy roadside restaurants scattered around the countryside. You will be able to find cheaper accommodation in Loulé than in the coastal towns and it is easy to get around and get to know the eastern Algarve by car from the town. The trails in the region offer great views and history.

WALK 1

Barrancos

Start/finish	Furnazinhas. Near the old primary school (white building) at the edge of the village. An Information board about the walk marks the beginning of the trail. (N37.363575, W7.576650)
Distance	8.5 km
Total ascent/descent	185m
Grade	2
Time	2hr 30min–3hr
Refreshments	Small bar in Furnazinhas village
Access	Furnazinhas is located on the M505 road which can be accessed from the N122 from the direction of Odeleite. There is a very limited bus service to and from the village and it may be difficult to reach the start of the walk by public transport. It is advisable to ask for information about buses in tourist offices. There are plenty of places to park near the school.

Start from the small village of Furnazinhas, where the way of life hasn't changed greatly over the years. Follow the wide tracks over tranquil hills with several stream crossings. Water only flows in these shallow streambeds during the wetter months. Views are dominated by hills populated by almond, olive and carob trees. The trail then follows a streambed back to the small village.

Facing the information board by the old primary school, go right on the tarmac road and a few metres later leave it on the yellow/red marked path by a wall to the right. The beginning of the trail is marked with a wooden arrow: PR10CTM 'Percurso Pedestre Barrancos' 7.8km. Follow the wide cobbled road uphill past some houses. It soon becomes a wide stony path with the buildings of Furnazinhas on your right.

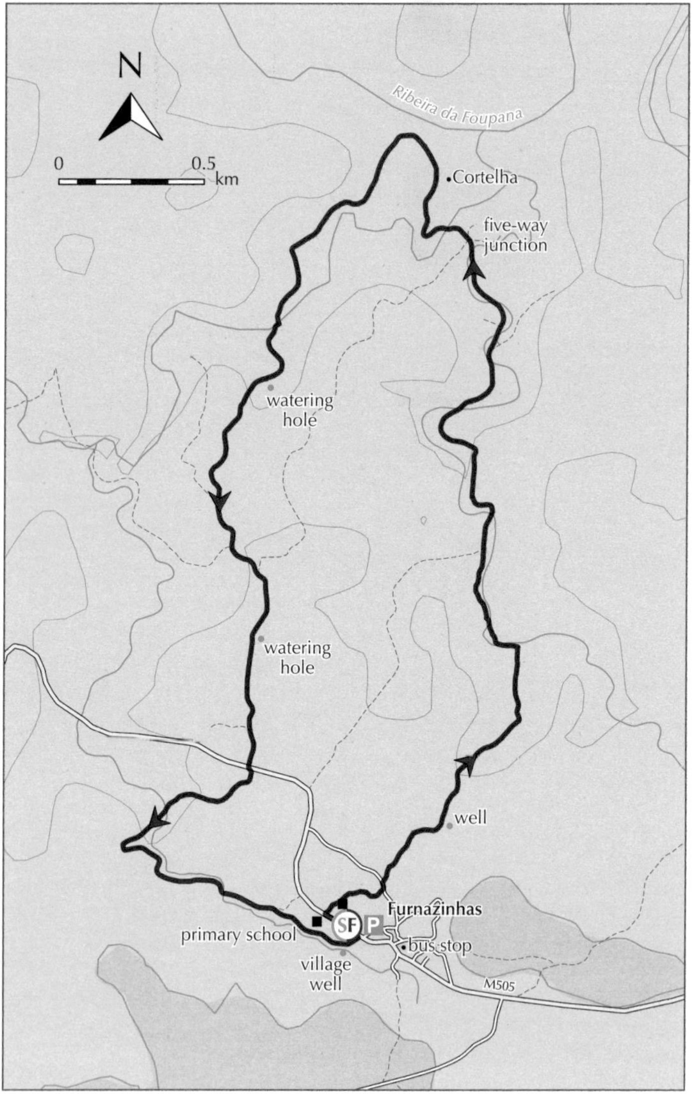
N
0
0.5
km
Ribeira da Foupana
Cortelha
five-way junction
watering hole
watering hole
well
Furnazinhas
primary school
bus stop
village well
M505

Soon join another track; keep left, and at the next junction take the middle path marked with a yellow/red sign. Leaving the houses behind, walk slightly downhill, with views dominated by the rolling hills in front of you. Pass a **well** and a trough and cross the streambed for the first time. Young pines grow on the nearby hills as you follow the wide stony path slightly downhill.

The trail crosses the streambed several times

Shortly after the first crossing, cross the streambed again and then continue alongside it. ▶

The path is lined with shrubs; notice the olive and carob trees near the path.

Leave the wide track on a narrow, slightly overgrown path to the left about 30min after starting the walk. Follow the familiar yellow/red signs along the streambed, which is overgrown with reeds.

Cross the streambed again, follow the overgrown path on its other side for about 50m and cross over again. Notice some cork oak, olive, almond and carob trees and soon you will see another yellow/red sign. Young pines dominate the nearby hills and a tiny building appears on the other side of the stream.

Reach a dirt track about 15min after joining the narrow path. Keep right. A few minutes later, at the junction take the dirt track on the right and almost immediately cross the streambed. Continue along the track lined with almond trees with views to the hills.

When a track joins, keep left slightly downhill. The path crosses the streambed twice in quick succession and then splits; keep left as the sign indicates.

Cross the streambed again, ignore the path on the left and continue straight on. Cross the streambed twice more and in front of you there is a ruin on the top of a low hill.

At the **five-way junction** carry straight on downhill, cross the streambed again and then continue slightly uphill. A track turns off to the right with a sign 'Cortelha 150m'. You can take a short detour to the ruins and rejoin the track a little further on. Alternatively carry straight on and a few minutes later pass the track with the 'Cortelha 170m' sign.

When the dirt track splits, keep left as the yellow/red sign indicates. ◂ Oak, almond and carob trees populate the hill near the track, and the low streambed is now on your left. When the track splits again, go left; soon crossing the streambed, then continue slightly uphill. Shortly, notice a hunter's high stand and a **watering hole** on your

There are olive trees near the track and you might notice a well between the shrubs.

left. A dirt track joins from the right; keep slightly left as the sign indicates. A few minutes later, ignore the track on the right, carry straight on slightly uphill and arrive at a junction, where you keep left towards Furnazinhas.

Ignore the track on the left and carry straight on as the white/yellow/red sign indicates. Near the track, you might notice some beehives on the hillside, and you soon pass a small **watering hole**. Ignore the path on the right and carry straight on with views of the hills stretching into the distance. Reach an asphalt road; the PR10 trail continues on its other side slightly to the left. You quickly pass a ramshackle building and a well to your right. When the path splits, keep left by the cultivated land and cross the streambed. Leave the dirt track to the left on a narrow path as the yellow/red sign indicates. Walk alongside a drystone wall, cross the streambed and then continue by a fence. At the junction keep right and about 20–30min after crossing the asphalt road, the trail runs between some houses. At the next junction take the PR10 CTM path to the left. Reach the tarmac road, keep left and a few metres later arrive back at the primary school.

Pine trees populate the low hills near Furnazinhas

WALK 2

Mina e Albufeira

Start/finish	Furnazinhas village centre. An information board marks the beginning of the trail. (N37.363095, W7.574657)
Distance	8km
Total ascent/descent	215m
Grade	2
Time	2hr 30min
Refreshments	Water and small shop in Furnazinhas, none along the way.
Access	Furnazinhas is located on the M505 road which can be accessed from the N122 road from the direction of Odeleite. There is a very limited bus service to and from the village and it may be difficult to reach the start of the walk by public transport. It is advisable to ask for information about buses in tourist offices. If you arrive by car, you can park in front of the school at the edge of the village. Facing the school building, go left and follow the tarmac road to the village centre.

From the small village of Furnazinhas, follow some dirt tracks to an old mine and then continue to the Odeleite reservoir. The hill-surrounded reservoir is a refreshing sight and an ideal spot for a picnic. Rolling low hills dominate the scenery as you follow this well-signposted trail.

An information board marks the beginning of the PR9CTM trail. Facing the bus stop, go left on the road and turn right on the next street as the yellow/red sign indicates. Walk between houses, and soon reach a tiny square with a fountain. Follow the yellow/red signs along a fence with a retaining wall on your right, eventually leaving the houses behind.

After about 10min, arrive at a **picnic area** beneath eucalyptus trees. Emerge onto a tarmac road and continue

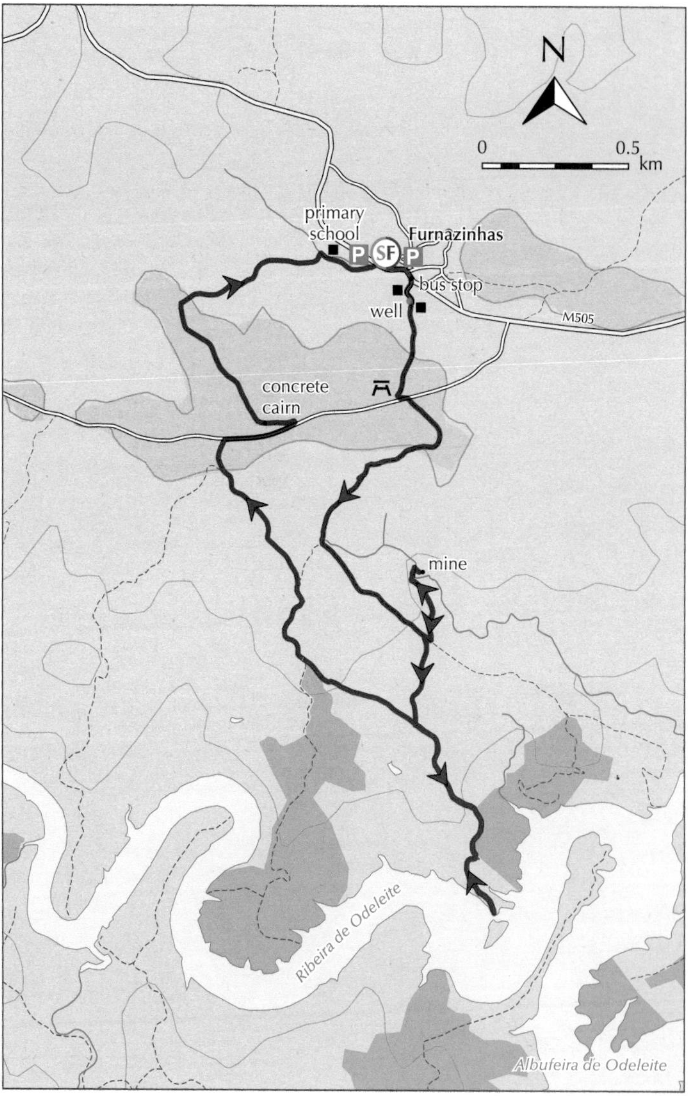
N
0
0.5
km
primary
school
P
SF
P
Furnazinhas
bus stop
well
M505
concrete
cairn
mine
Ribeira de Odeleite
Albufeira de Odeleite

The nearby hills are scattered with young pines and you might notice a trough on the left.

on its other side slightly left on a dirt track. Ignore the track on the left and carry straight on. When the track splits into three, follow the middle track downhill. ◂ At the junction, go left as the yellow/red sign indicates. Rolling hills fill the horizon while there is a gully on the left and soon you have the first glimpse of the reservoir, surrounded by small hills.

About 30–40min after starting the trail, arrive at a junction. There is a sign: *Mina* 270m to the left, and Albufeira 1.3km to the right.

First take the left path to the *mina* (**mine**). It is a short detour, following a slightly overgrown path downhill for about 10min. Arrive at an overgrown area and look out for the mine – a small tunnel cut into rocks.

Retrace your steps back to the junction and continue (right and then left) towards Albufeira. At the next junction go left as the Albufeira 890m sign indicates (you will be following the dirt track on the right towards Furnazinhas 3.5km after the detour to the reservoir). As you descend, you will have more and more views of the reservoir.

Slowly descending towards the Odeleite reservoir

Odeleite reservoir: a great place for a picnic

Ignore the dirt track on the right and carry straight on as it bends slightly left.

Arrive at the reservoir about 20min after the junction with the Albufeira 890m sign. It is a great place to stop for a rest or picnic before retracing your steps back to the junction with the signs. ▸

Odeleite reservoir was built between 1992 and 1998 and is the biggest reservoir in south east Portugal.

From the junction, follow the dirt track towards Furnazinhas 3.5km. ▸ Ignore the dirt track joining from the left and carry straight on. In the distance on the left you can see the building on a hill which you might have noticed on the way there. Ignore the track on the right going downhill, and a few minutes later one on the left, and keep on the yellow/red marked track. Emerge onto a tarmac road, go right and follow it with views of the hills and reservoir in the distance. About 5min later, leave the tarmac road on a path to the left. Go uphill on the dirt track, and pass a **concrete cairn**. The track undulates for about 15min. At a small junction at the edge of the village keep right and walk back to the village centre. When you reach the tarmac road in the village, turn left and walk back to the school building with the parking area.

Low hills fill the horizon.

WALK 3

Masmorra trail

Start/finish	Mealha village (N37.363479, W7.871427)
Distance	6.5km
Total ascent/descent	155m
Grade	1
Time	2hr
Refreshments	None along the trail.
Access	Mealha village is located on the M504 road about 9km northwest of Cachopo. There are plenty of places to park near the bus stop in Mealha, from where a handful of signposted trails start. Buses are infrequent.

A signposted trail taking you past traditional roundhouses and a megalithic burial site with good views along the route.

Start walking along the tarmac road, following the PR8TVR Masmorra (6km) sign. Follow the yellow/red signs between the houses and when the road splits, go right on the dirt track. There are houses on the right and almond trees on the left. Soon you walk by some pens and then before long back to houses. Take the first left on a wide stony track and soon pass a **round house**.

The small circular buildings are called **palheiros**. They were used to store tools or hay for animals; however there is evidence that they were also used for housing. The roof was made from hay or reeds and the walls from slate. The size was usually 0.5m wide, 2.5m high and 6m in diameter. There are plenty of examples of these buildings in Mealha where there is an information board giving more information about Portugal's traditional round stone buildings.

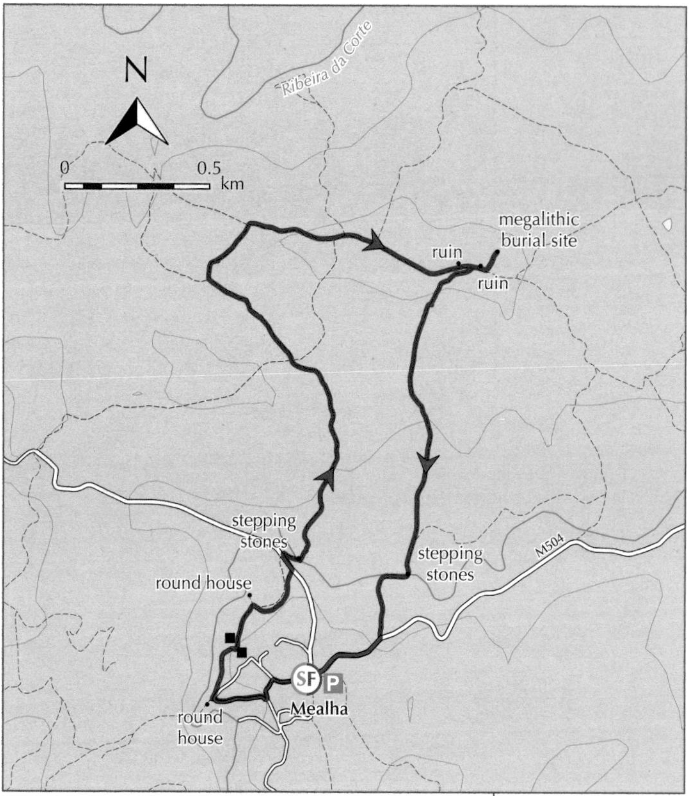

At the junction, in front of you there is another **round house**; you can take a closer look, but the route continues to the right. ▶ Continue along the dirt track and a few minutes later reach a tarmac road. Go left on this road and a few metres later leave it to the right as the sign indicates. Descend to the streambed, cross it (there are **stepping stones** to help the crossing if necessary) and continue on the dirt track between drystone walls.

Yellow/red signs mark the trail.

Ignore a track joining from the right, and a few minutes later another from the left, and carry straight on. ▶

The hillside is scattered with almond trees and pines.

Megalithic burial site

The dirt track goes under a high voltage wire and then continues slightly uphill. At the junction, carry straight on slightly downhill, following the PR8 sign. A few minutes later, keep right uphill and arrive at a junction; go right. Ignore any tracks joining from the left and right and continue straight on and soon notice a **ruin** in front of you. As you pass the ruin, you can also see the village on the right. Near a second, smaller, **ruin** there is a path going downhill towards the village. Before following this, take a detour to the **megalithic burial site**. Follow the dirt track a bit further, straight on and look out for the information board on the left side of the road. Near this information board there is a narrow path which takes you to the burial site. ◂

This megalithic burial site was probably built during the 3rd or 4th millennium BC.

Views to the low hills

Retrace your steps to the small junction near the **ruins**, and go downhill towards the village. Yellow/red signs mark the trail. The houses of Mealha and wind turbines on the nearby hill dominate the views. The track might be slightly overgrown here, but it is still clearly visible and easy to follow. At the junction, continue straight on downhill towards the village.

The dirt track soon goes under the high voltage wire again. Ignore two dirt tracks joining from the left in quick succession and carry straight on. Soon a dirt track joins from the right, but carry straight on. ▶ Cross the streambed (there are **stepping stones** to help the crossing if there is water in the stream) and walk alongside some cultivated land. Emerge onto the tarmac road, keep right and follow the tarmac road for 6–8min back to the village.

There are vines by the track.

WALK 4

Cerro dos Negros

Start/finish	Sol e Serra snack bar, Corte Garcia (N37.199000, W7.973560)
Distance	6.5km
Total ascent/descent	250m
Grade	2 (short walk, but there is a steep ascent and descent)
Time	2hr
Refreshments	Snack bar at the beginning and at the end of the trail but take plenty of water with you especially if it is a hot day.
Access	The Sole e Serra snack bar, just outside Corte Garcia is located on the N396 road about 10km north of Loulé.

This short, circular trail takes you up to the Cerro dos Negros, 404m. From the small peak the views are dominated by green and brown hills dotted with white houses. On a clear day you can see as far as the Monchique range. This is a well-signposted route with a short but constant climb to the top and a very steep downhill return.

Yellow/red signs mark this trail.

Facing the **Sole e Serra** snack bar with the information board on your left, follow the tarmac road to the right. ◄ About 100m later, opposite the bus stop, leave the tarmac road to the right. A wooden arrow (Serra e Montes PR13LLE) indicates the direction. This narrow tarmac road is marked with a yellow/red sign. Just before reaching some houses, turn left as signposted and follow the dirt track downhill. A few minutes later, cross a streambed then continue uphill. When the track splits, keep right, heading slightly downhill.

Continue on the cork oak-lined track along the streambed. Soon cross the streambed again, and immediately after, ignore the dirt track on the right and carry straight on. Cork oaks populate the hills. A few minutes later ignore the dirt track on the right and carry straight on downhill

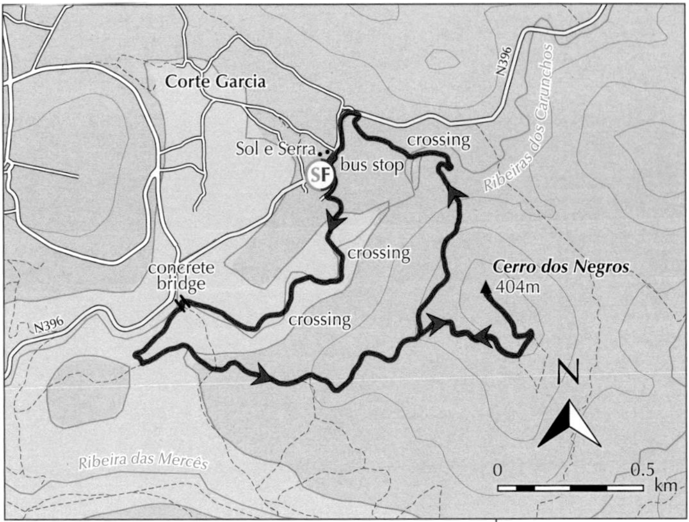

with the streambed on your left. Arrive at a **concrete bridge** about 30min after starting from the restaurant. (The track on the right leads to the main road.) Keep left and cross the bridge. Immediately after the bridge there is a junction; keep right as the yellow/red sign indicates and follow the stony forest track uphill. On the right you may spot the main road, but soon the track swings away from it.

At the next junction, go left uphill. The houses of Corte Garcia nestled on the hill dominate the views on the left and hills fill the horizon on your right. At the next junction carry straight on (following the middle track) as the Cerro dos Negros sign indicates. At the next split, ignore the track on the right and carry straight on uphill. You can admire the views as you ascend. When the track splits, keep right uphill. Follow this track to the top. You will be climbing constantly for about 15min. From the top (**Cerro dos Negros**, 404m) a panorama of endless hills dotted with small villages unfolds. You can recognise the Rocha da Pena and on a clear day you can see as far as the Monchique range.

Views from Cerro dos Negros

Shrubs and cork oaks populate the hill.

From the top, retrace your steps back to the junction and continue to the right. You can find the yellow/red signs on rocks. ◂ Ignore the track going steeply downhill on the left and carry straight on. Follow the very steep forest track downhill for about 10min. Ignore the track on the right, carry straight on then **cross** a streambed. Soon spot a building on your left and then emerge onto a tarmac road about 45min after leaving the peak. The signposted trail continues on the other side of the road, but turn left and follow the tarmac road for about 350m back to the starting point.

WALK 5

Fonte Benémola

Start/finish	About 1.5km west of Querença. An information board marks the beginning of the trail. (N37.198621, W8.004421)
Distance	4km
Total ascent/descent	45m
Grade	1
Time	1hr 15min
Refreshments	None along the trail
Access	M524 road about 1.5km west of Querença. The parking area and the start of the trail is signposted on the M524 road. There are plenty of places to park at the beginning of the trail.

This is a well-signposted trail in a protected valley, with helpful boards along the track providing information about the local plants, wildlife and human activity in the area. Allow some time to stop by the attractive stream.

The PR16LLE marked trail starts from the parking area. Follow the wide dirt track and soon you can hear the trickling water from the shallow valley on the left. Walk along the retaining wall and ignore two paths in quick succession on the left, staying on the wide track marked with white/yellow/red signs. Notice some buildings on the hillside and pass a **parking area**.

Benémola river is one of the very few rivers in the Algarve that carries water all year round. The protected **Fonte Benémola** is home to a wide variety of plants and flowers.

Ignore the small path on the right, and keep to the dirt track which crosses the stream. About 15–20min after

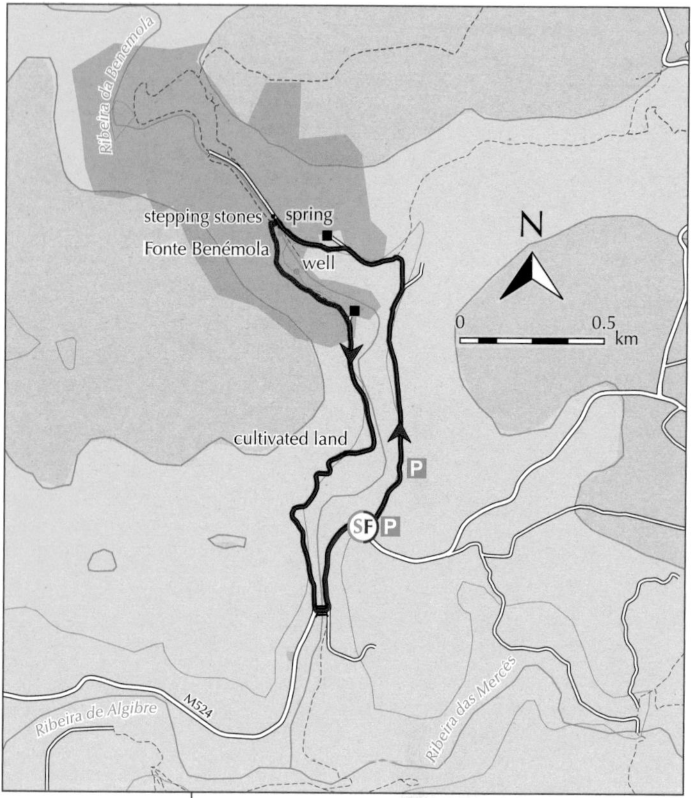

starting the trail, arrive at a junction with an information board. Keep left towards Fonte de Benémola. Continue along the dirt track, ignoring the path going downhill from the information board. Follow the sign towards Fonte Benémola. Ignore the path by the barn and pass some buildings.

Follow the yellow/red signs slightly downhill, and shortly arrive at the trickling stream among trees, and a picnic area by the dirt track. Just before the picnic tables, keep left, and descend on the steps to the stream. Cross the stream on the **stepping stones** and keep left on its other side. There is cultivated land on the left. Ignore the small path on the right and continue on the wide track. ▶

Notice the old *'nora'* (old well) on the left hand side: you can take a closer look before you continue on the wide track.

Pass a building by the dirt track. On the left you can see the building near the beginning of the trail on the other side of the valley. There is **cultivated land** on the left and cork trees grow by the track. Ignore the track on the right and continue on the dirt track. Join another dirt track, keep left and emerge onto a tarmac road. Go left and cross a **bridge**. Keep left after the bridge and follow the tarmac road for about 10min and arrive back at the car park where the trail started.

Walker crossing the stream

WALK 6

Rocha da Pena

Start/finish	Penina village (N37.249809, W8.114624)
Distance	7.5km
Total ascent/total descent	250m
Grade	2
Time	2hr 30min
Refreshments	Bar in Penina, and snack bar in the hamlet of Rocha
Access	Penina is 7.5km west of Salir. Penina is located on the M1094 road. There is a limited bus service from Loulé. Seek information locally.

The Rocha da Pena is a protected area where local guides take small groups in the hope of spotting birds or to marvel at the wildflowers. This circular, signposted trail offers some fine views to the nearby hills, as well as to Penina and towards the coast. You can also admire a defensive Iron Age wall and an old well along the trail.

The yellow/red signposted trail starts near the **bus stop** in the small village of Penina. Here you can find an information board, and a small bar near the bus stop. There are also some toilets located further down the tarmac road.

Start uphill at the bend in the road on Travessa Candido Guerrerio street. Follow the yellow/red signs between the houses of Penina. Soon you pass the *Mini Museo* (**mini museum**) and then continue uphill as the yellow/red sign indicates. A few minutes later you will be leaving the houses behind. Pass a circular water tank and arrive at a barrier. After the barrier, the concrete track changes into a wide stony track. Pass a ruin on the right, and ignore the track on the left. Continue uphill, ignoring the path on the right immediately after the ruin.

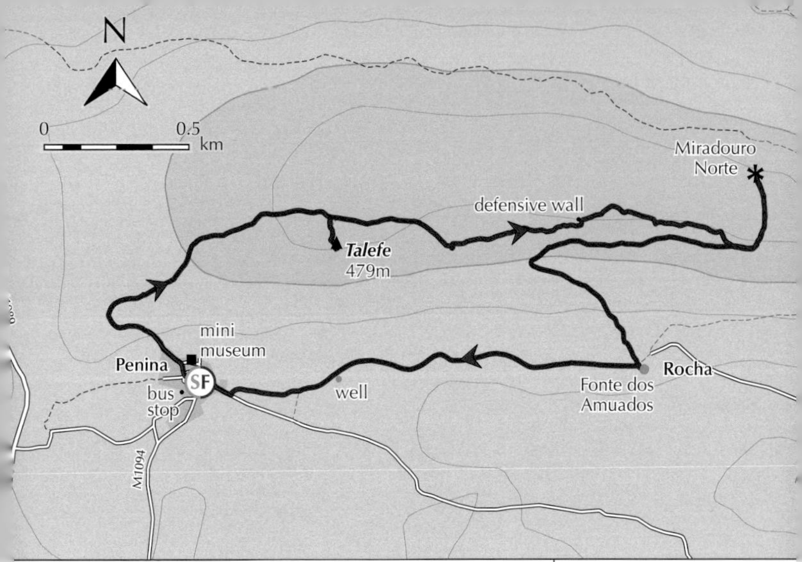

Ignore any side tracks and follow the marked, rocky track uphill. It is regularly lined with oak trees, shrubs and rocks, and carob trees and juniper grow on the hillside. As you climb, you can enjoy more and more views of the rolling hills.

About 30–40min after starting from the village, arrive at a wooden sign: Talefe, 479m. From here take the short detour to the **Talefe** peak. Follow the narrow path on the right and a few minutes later reach the peak, marked with a concrete cairn.

Enjoy the panoramic views of the Barrocal (limestone region) of Loulé and then retrace your steps to the sign and keep right on the wide stony track.

Part of the Iron Age **defensive wall** appears in front of you in the distance. The path levels out a bit in an open area and then it narrows down. A narrow path on the right takes you to a viewpoint from where you can see the rock face of Rocha da Pena to the right. ▸

This rock face is popular with climbers.

Continue on the path, bordered by rosemary, shrubs and juniper, and you almost always have views to the surrounding hills. From the well-signposted trail numerous narrow paths lead out to rocky outcrops from where more

The rock face of Rocha da Pena

generous views can be enjoyed. At the junction, carry straight on slightly uphill as the sign indicates.

About 30–40min after leaving Talefe peak, arrive at the **defensive wall**. The path continues by the information board. The remainder of the wall stretches far into the distance on the hillside.

> Originally there were two **defensive walls**, dating back to the Iron Age and also used by the Moors, but only one is visible today. The Moors hid out in the Rocha da Pena area during the Christian reconquest of Portugal, when Alfonso III (1248–79) claimed back the area – making him the first to claim the title of King of Portugal and the Algarve. (However, fighting with the Muslims continued and it was only in the late 13th century that the Portuguese secured the area.)

Shortly after the defensive wall, pass an information board about the local flora. The narrow rocky path continues among shrubs, slightly downhill and a few minutes later arrives at a junction. Continue straight on towards the Miradouro Norte. Ignore a track on the right and about 10min from the junction arrive at **Miradouro Norte**. From here you can enjoy some fine views to northern Belevedere. Drink in the views and retrace your steps to the junction with the Miradouro Norte sign. Keep left downhill.

As you descend, you might notice some paths running towards the rocks; these are used by climbers to access the climbing routes.

About 20min after starting the descent from the junction, arrive at a concrete road at the hamlet of Rocha. Emerge onto the concrete track by a small snack bar. There is a parking area with a fountain (**Fonte dos Amuados**) but a warning sign on the tap informs that the water might not be suitable for drinking. However, the bar offers refreshments.

Keep right and the tarmac road changes back to a dirt track. Pass some buildings; occasional yellow/red signs mark this section of the trail. Notice the **old well** on the left side of the road about 15–20min after leaving the hamlet of Rocha da Pena.

Watering the crops was always important in the Algarve, which has only a small amount of rainfall throughout the year. The Arabs who came to the Iberian Peninsula in the 8th century brought their technologies for raising, storing and channelling water and built *noras* (**old wells**). The name *nora* comes from the Arabic word *noura* and means gearwheel for raising water. As a donkey walked in circles turning the wheel, a container dipped into the water, emerged full and then gravity tipped the water into a trough and the empty container dipped back into the water. As a walker you can see many unused, abandoned '*noras*' in the countryside.

Leave the track to the right by a fence soon after the 'Most common species' information board. Keeping the fence to your left, follow this narrow path and a few minutes later pass some buildings and arrive at a dirt track. Keep left and emerge onto a tarmac road. Go right and a few minutes later arrive back at the bus stop where the trail started.

Looking back towards the village of Penina

WALK 7

Paderne castle

Start/finish	Paderne castle car park (N37.157220, W8.200000)
Alternative start/finish	Small car park under A22 motorway, by the river. (N37.160100, W8.201053)
Distance	3.5km
Total ascent/descent	50m
Grade	1
Time	1hr starting from the castle, plus allow some time to spend in the castle if possible.
Refreshments	None along the way
Access	Travelling from east to west on the N270 road go left after the cemetery in Paderne at the Fonte de Paderne, Castello sign. Follow the road to the Fonte and after that, take the dirt track on the right, following the Castello sign. Follow this dirt track to the parking area under the A22 motorway. There is ample parking here, or continue all the way up to the castle ruins where there are also plenty of parking places.

This short trail includes many historical sites. If you are lucky enough to visit when the castle is open (opening hours are not publicised), you can explore the courtyard; otherwise you can admire the exterior and enjoy the views from the castle hill. Follow the narrow path along the Quarteira river, and stop for a picnic by the ancient stone bridge. There are information boards about the plants and wildlife located along the path.

From the car park under the motorway

Head towards the castle, go left on the dirt track and follow it uphill. When the track splits, keep right and about 300m later ignore the road joining from the left and ascend to the castle.

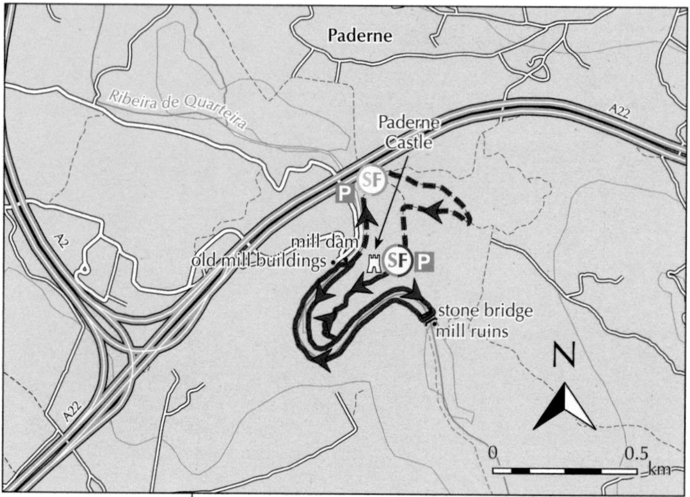

Information boards about plants are located along the path.

Facing the **castle**, keep left and walk along the wall. A yellow/red sign marks the narrow path. At the end of the wall carry straight on, on the shrub-lined stony path. You can enjoy great views to the hills and the lush valley. (Only a few minutes after the start, if you look back, you have a great view of the ruin perched on the hill top.) Descend for about 10min and arrive at a junction. Go left on the narrow path (you will be returning to this junction on the path from the right, even though it is marked with a yellow/red cross.)

Follow the narrow, shrub-lined path – marked with yellow/red signs – along the streambed. The streambed is on your right. ◂ About 10min after joining the path by the stream, arrive at a junction with a **stone bridge**. There is a picnic area here and an information board about a mill. Continue to the right, cross the stone bridge and then keep right as the sign indicates. The view is dominated by the castle on the top of the hill. The narrow path is more overgrown on this side of the stream, but several information boards about plants, the area, butterflies, and the stream are located along the path. About 20min after

The remains of the church within the walls of Paderne castle

crossing the stone bridge, the path splits. The yellow/red marked path goes uphill to the left. However, continue along the stream straight on, even though this path is marked with a yellow/red cross.

You will arrive at another information board near an old **watermill**. The building is private property, respect the signs and stay out of its grounds. Walk along the building and see a small **mill dam**. Cross over the streambed by the dam, and arrive at another information board. There are picnic benches and a route map here. ▶ After crossing the stream, keep sharply right towards the castle. The streambed is on your right again,

If you parked under the motorway, then keep left and a few minutes later arrive back at the parking area.

An old watermill by a small dam

and the path is wider here. You might notice a small ruin, and there are more information boards along the trail. Rustling reeds and bird song entertain you, carob and olive trees populate the area. About 10–12min after crossing the stream, arrive at a junction, go left and climb back to the castle.

Paderne castle is believed to be one of the seven castles on the Portuguese flag, representing those taken by the Portuguese from the Moors in the Algarve. It was built as a Moorish fort and in 1248 conquered by the army of the Portuguese King Alfonso III.

The castle lost its strategic importance during the 16th century and in 1755 when an earthquake destroyed part of it, the people moved to the present location of Paderne village. The church in the castle, the age of which is unknown, was also damaged by the earthquake.

CENTRAL REGION

The final stretch to the top of Picota (Walk 11)

CENTRAL REGION

Silves, with its castle, is clearly visible in the distance on Walk 8

The central region offers a variety of trails, from the slopes of Fóia – the highest peak in the Algarve, which dominates the Central region (Walk 10)– to a *levada* walk near Silves (Walk 8) and a forest walk from Barao de São João (Walk 17). From the snaking trails on the slopes of Fóia, extensive views can be enjoyed towards the coast. There has been a spa since Roman times in **Caldas de Monchique**, and the 19th century village is well visited but it still has a relaxed and peaceful atmosphere. You can climb Picota – the second-highest peak in the Algarve – from Caldas de Monchique and then descend to **Monchique** village (Walk 11). The village is usually bustling with tourists, but you can climb Fóia from here.

The village can also be a great base for those wishing to explore the trails in the area. You can find accommodation both in Monchique and Caldas de Monchique, but given the latter's popularity as a spa destination, it can get busy. There are shops, cafes and restaurants in both villages, however Monchique might be the better bet for walkers.

A castle, perched on a small hill in Silves, comes into view when you follow the *levada* along the Arade River (Walk 8). **Silves** town is worth a visit; the narrow streets near the castle can be explored in an afternoon stroll. There are plenty of hotels, cafés and restaurants in the town if you are planning to stay for a few days. Several trails can easily be reached from Silves if you have your own transport.

The small, quiet, village of **Marmelete** is known for its *medronho*, the traditional Algarve fire water. A meandering trail, on the slopes populated with cork oaks, starts from the village (Walk 14).

WALK 8

Levada trail

Start/finish	Mira Rio restaurant after Falacho village, near Silves (N37.187094, W8.487551)
Distance	6.5km
Total ascent/descent	110m
Grade	1
Time	2hr–2hr 15min
Refreshments	Mira Rio restaurant at the start and finish.
Access	Mira Rio restaurant is located on the N124 road about 4km west of Silves. There are plenty of places to park in front of the Mira Rio restaurant.

Follow the narrow, meandering water channel near the river. Stroll past citrus orchards and watch a flock of storks searching for their dinner, where the Odelouca and Arade rivers meet. On the return section you can enjoy some great views of the surrounding hills. The trail is not signposted; however, it is easy to follow.

Facing the **Mira Rio restaurant**, go left on the tarmac road. A few minutes later, leave the road on the first dirt track to the right near the ruin of a house. When you reach the *levada* (irrigation channel), go sharply left and then continue along the water channel. Pass a ruin of a house, on your left, and a few minutes after joining the *levada*, cross a narrow tarmac road. (You can access the water channel from this road as well). Continue on the other side of the road, along the water channel, with lime orchards and plantations on your right. There are a few houses on the left as the levada gets close to a small tarmac road, but soon you have better views to the river and low hills. ▸ The path gets close to the **Odelouca river**, but vegetation often obstructs the views.

On the right you can make out the silhouette of Fóia and Picota.

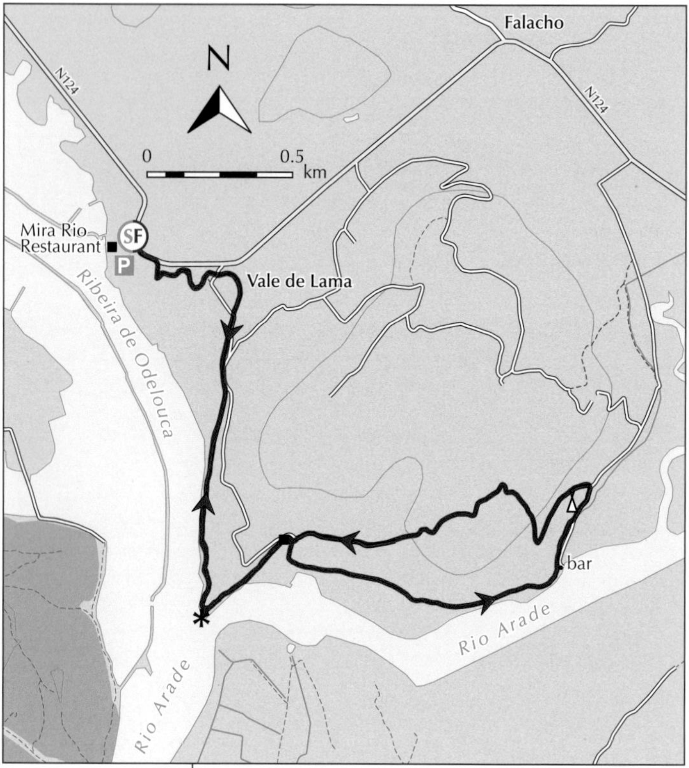

Despite the trail passing close to a settlement and plantations, it occasionally feels remote as you can only see a rocky hillside and the *levada* as you walk along the reed-lined path. Pass an overflow spillway and cross a small bridge, then continue with the water channel on your right. You might notice an old gate on your left. About 30min after joining the levada, cross a small concrete bridge and look out for a tiny path which takes you to a **viewpoint** on some rocks, beneath a eucalyptus tree by the river. The **Odelouca** and **Arade** rivers meet here, and it is a great place to stop and watch storks and other birds.

There are great views to the Arade River

Continue along the meandering *levada* by the river, with low hills in the background. Soon notice some houses on the right. Curve around the **house** on your right and at the end of the building notice a track on the left (you will be returning on that track). However, continue alongside the water channel and soon Portimão and the bridge near the coast in the distance come into view. Soon Silves castle and its houses perched on the small hillside by the river also appear in the distance. You pass a small **bar** by the river and then the water channel disappears under the path for a few metres. Arrive at a dirt track about an hour into the walk, and keep left uphill by a house.

There is a **caravan campsite** on the left and when the tarmac road splits, go left uphill and pass the campsite's reception. After the reception the road becomes a dirt track, and when it splits, keep right uphill with great views to the river. At the dirt track junction, go left. There is an electricity pole on the hill on your left. Ignore the dirt track joining from the left, and keep right uphill. At the junction, go left (the right track goes towards a farm) and you can enjoy the views towards Picota and Fóia. Ignore the track on the left and carry straight on.

Excellent **views** accompany you on this section. The meandering Arade River dominates the views on your right and you can spot the small viewpoint with the tiny islet nearby. On a clear day you can see all the way to the ocean and Portimão.

The nearby hillsides are scattered with houses, and as you descend you pass under an electric wire. The dirt track becomes a narrow tarmac road and arrives back at the *levada*. Turn right and retrace your steps along the water channel to the roadside restaurant.

The levada *channels water to the cultivated lands*

WALK 9

Fonte Santa

Start/finish	Roadside about 1km west of Odelouca dam. Wooden sign marks the beginning of the trail. (N37.288470, W8.485465)
Distance	4km
Total ascent/descent	125m
Grade	1
Time	1hr 30min
Refreshments	None along the way
Access	From Odelouca village (N124), take the road towards Alferce on the west of the Odelouca river heading north. After about 14km turn right towards the Odelouca dam and Fonte Santa. You can park along the road.

This short trail – part of the GR13 – follows a stream through a forest to an old 'bath house'. A concert of frogs, bird-song, buzzing bees, rustling leaves and trickling water entertains you along the trail. From the bath house you can return the same way or add a short extension and admire the surrounding hills.

A wooden arrow indicates where the dirt track leaves the tarmac. Start on this marked track downhill from the road. Shortly you will notice a stream on your left. The forest track runs beneath trees, along the stream and in front of you the views are dominated by hills. When the forest track splits (left goes to the bushes) keep right as the white/red sign indicates.

Ignore the track on the left (which runs towards a house on the hill) and continue straight on. Cross the stream over some rocks and then pass a small **picnic area**. Ignore the track on the left, and cross the stream again over some rocks. Shortly you will cross the stream again; bear left and take the right path as the white/red

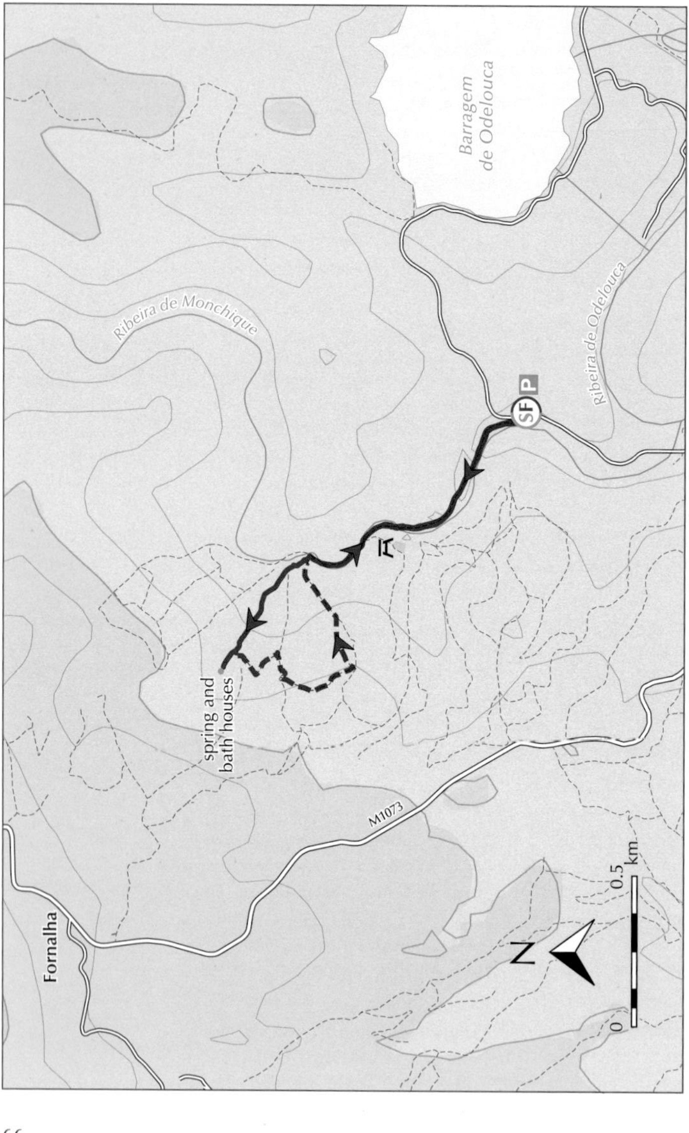
Barragem
de Odelouca
Ribeira de Monchique
Ribeira de Odelouca
SF
P
spring and
bath houses
M1073
Fornalha
N
0
0.5
km

GR13 sign indicates. The narrow stony path runs uphill with views to the hills. Ignore the path on the left (which is marked with a white/red cross) and continue straight on as the 'GR' sign indicates. ▶

From down below you can hear the sound of trickling water.

Descend back to the now narrow stream and cross it. Then walk slightly uphill again with the stream on your left and arrive at a stone building. Walk alongside the building; the GR-marked trail goes left, but if you would like to visit the **bath houses**, carry straight on alongside the other buildings. In the last building you can see some small pools with trickling water.

Fonte Santa – the hidden hot spring in the south of Picota – is believed to have healing properties. Although no concrete dates are known, the oldest of the crumbling bath houses were probably built at the beginning of the 19th century and the others at the beginning of the 20th. It is believed that the site was visited well before that, and people still make trips to the site. Some records suggest that it had been visited by kings of Portugal and Italy.

The hot spring can be found at the end of the building

Views to the hills near Fonte Santa

Retrace your steps to the small junction where the GR13 path – marked with white/red – goes right (if you are coming from the bath house).

From here you can either retrace your steps to the tarmac road or add a short extension to the walk to enjoy views of the hills.

Extension

From the bath house buildings take the GR13 path, cross the stream, and go uphill. Almost immediately you have some views to the surrounding hills on your left.

Soon, join a wide path and keep right (to the left it is marked with a cross). Follow this wide path uphill (a narrow path marked with white/red leaves the track to the left, but a few metres further on rejoins the same wide path). Ignore the track on the right and follow the contour of the hillside with views to the hills. On the left you can see the Odelouca Dam surrounded by low hills. At a junction, go left downhill on the first wide path. (The GR13 continues to the right and this time you have to take the path marked with a white/red cross!). ◂ Ignore the track on the right and head straight downhill. It is very steep all the way down. Arrive back at the stream, go right and retrace your steps to the tarmac road.

It is a very steep downhill section on a loose surface!

WALK 10

Monchique–Fóia loop

Start/finish	Monchique centre (N37.317977, W-8.556558)
Distance	13km
Total ascent/descent	615m
Grade	3
Time	3hr 30min–4hr
Refreshments	Cafés/restaurants in Monchique village, snack bar at the top of Fóia, and two restaurants along the return section
Access	Monchique village is located on the N266 road, less than 30km north of Portimão. There are buses from Portimão but check the timetable with the local tourist office. If you are driving, there are plenty of places to park near the village centre.

From the small bustling centre of Monchique, climb up to the highest mountain in the Algarve. Fóia is popular: visitors can drive up to the peak, and coachloads of tourists arrive daily to admire the views. The first section of the trail described is part of a long distance trail, Via Algarviana, marked GR13 (white/red). It passes an old convent and then follows footpaths. Fóia's peak is dotted with many antennas and therefore might not be the most attractive summit, but you can enjoy the great panorama and the excellent views along the way.

The start of the trail is marked by an information board on the main square in the centre of Monchique village. From the square, follow Rua do Porto Fundo, marked with a brown walker sign. Ascend the stairs between bars and shops and leave this wide street to the left on Travessa das Guerreiras. A white/red GR sign marks this turn. This narrow street runs uphill between colourful buildings. At the junction, carry straight on as the brown walker sign and an arrow indicate. Follow the white/red sign to the left and then keep right uphill just before the fountain. Continue

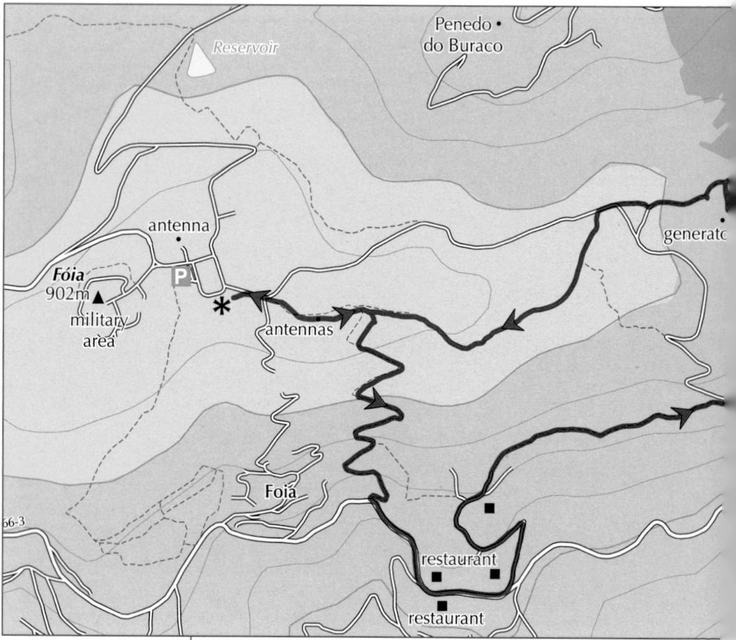

uphill as the GR13 sign indicates and when the road splits, go left uphill by the building with the CMM 1952 sign.

Follow the tarmac road along a fence, which then turns into a stony path. The everyday noises from the village can still be heard as you walk among cork oaks, and a few minutes after leaving the houses behind arrive at the old **Nossa Senhora do Desterro convent**.

Nossa Senhora do Desterro Convent was founded in 1631 by Pero da Silva who was the governor of Portuguese India from where he brought the ivory image of Our Lady. It is also believed that the governor might have been buried at the convent. According to a different legend, two sailors vowed that they would build a church on Portuguese land if they survived the challenging seas.

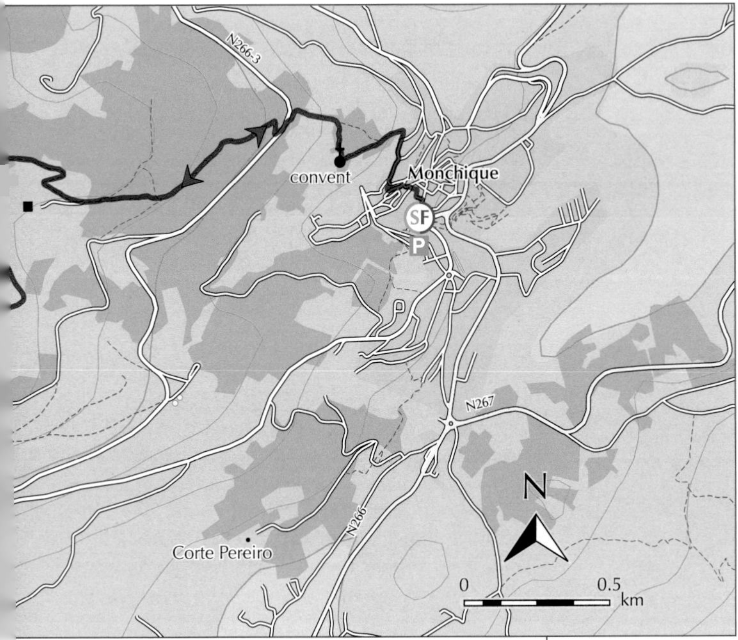

The convent was given to the Franciscan Order. The 1755 earthquake destroyed it, but it was later rebuilt. The building has been deteriorating over the years. Plans have been made for restoration, however lack of money has prevented any work being carried out.

A friendly man might be there to invite you in to see the inside of the convent. He doesn't own the building, but it appears that he is using part of it and the enclosed yard. If he is there and invites you in, then take the opportunity to see the walls from the inside as well.

Otherwise, when you reach the building, continue uphill to the right with the walls – decorated with private signs – on your left.

After the convent, notice three small paths between trees, and take the left uphill. Follow the white/red signs as the path swings left. Emerge onto a tarmac road, keep left and about 60m later leave this tarmac road on a path – marked with a white/red sign – to the right.

Pines, young eucalyptus, and thorny gorse grow on the hillside.

When the path splits, keep left. ◂ Ignore any tracks joining from the left or right and continue on the well-trodden path with views to Picota and the surrounding hills on the left, and on a clear day you can see all the way to the coast.

Arrive at a forest track about 15min after leaving the tarmac road and keep right. Ignore a track on the right and continue straight on. There is a house on your left on the hillside and when the forest track splits, keep right. You will see some houses scattered on the hillside. Ignore an overgrown track on the right and continue on the well-trodden track. Pass some houses and cultivated land and as you are ascending enjoy the views towards Picota.

There are huge rocks by the track.

About 40–50min after leaving the old convent, arrive at a track junction. The yellow/red marked PR3MCQ Trilho da Fóia joins from the left. Continue straight on as the GR13 sign indicates. (You will be returning to this junction on the PR3MCQ route.) ◂ Soon leave the forest track on a small path uphill to the right. The peak of Fóia with its antennas appears in front of you.

A few minutes later, emerge onto a tarmac road and keep right towards the antennas, but a few metres later leave this tarmac road to the left for a narrow, unmarked path. The peak is in view as you walk between shrubs and you also have great views to Picota and the distant coast. The path splits twice in quick succession (the left path is very overgrown), keep right both times. Arrive at the **antennas**. The path continues to the left marked yellow/red, but first, walk right towards the other antennas to the peak area. There is a **car park**, a snack bar, toilet and souvenir shop here on the Algarve's highest peak.

Enjoy some great views from the peak and retrace your steps back to the junction where you arrived at the antennas. Keep right as the yellow/red sign indicates (you arrived on the left path). You will be following the trail

marked PR3MCQ (yellow/red). Descend steeply downhill with views to the coast. ▶

Juniper grows by the path.

About 30min after leaving the peak, pass some houses and then emerge onto a tarmac road. Go left and follow this road. Walk past two roadside **restaurants**, and about 10min after joining the tarmac road, leave it to the left on a forest track by a house. Follow this stony track uphill with views to Picota on your right. Ignore the path first on right then on the left and follow the forest track as it bends right uphill.

There is a house on the left on the terraced hillside. When the track splits, keep left and pass a villa, and then after the building go uphill as the yellow/red sign indicates. ▶ Walk past a pen and continue to ascend. Fig, chestnut and eucalyptus trees populate the hillside. Ignore the path on the right, carry straight on and when you reach a tarmac road, cross over and on its other side continue straight on. There is a small building on the left side of the track and more views open up on the right. The hillside is scattered with houses. Leave the forest track on a path to the left uphill. Keep right by the **generator** house building as the yellow/red signs indicates. Arrive at a junction about 50min after leaving the tarmac road. This is the junction from which you headed to Fóia. Keep right now and retrace your steps back to Monchique.

You will have views to Picota on the right.

WALK 11

Caldas de Monchique to Picota and to Monchique

Start	Caldas de Monchique's centre (N37.285961, W8.553571)
Finish	Monchique
Alternative finish	Caldas de Monchique
Distance	12km
Total ascent	550m
Total descent	305m
Grade	3
Time	4hr
Refreshments	Restaurants and cafés in Caldas de Monchique and in Monchique. None along the trail.
Access	Caldas de Monchique is located on the N66 road about 20km north of Portimão. There is plenty of parking in Caldas de Monchique. Buses run from Portimão, but check the timetable with the local tourist office. There are limited buses from Monchique at the end of the walk, but walkers should check information and timetables locally. Taxis are also available.

The trail follows some paths which are popular with mountain bikers, so extra care should be taken in case you meet one riding down the path. However, it is a far more scenic route than the one suggested in the leaflets available from the tourist office. From the Algarve's second-highest peak you can enjoy some magnificent views, then descend to Monchique where you can wander through the cobbled streets and relax in the cafés.

There has been a spa in **Caldas de Monchique** since Roman times. The small 19th century village and the thermal spa are well-visited, but Caldas de Monchique still has a relaxed and peaceful atmosphere.

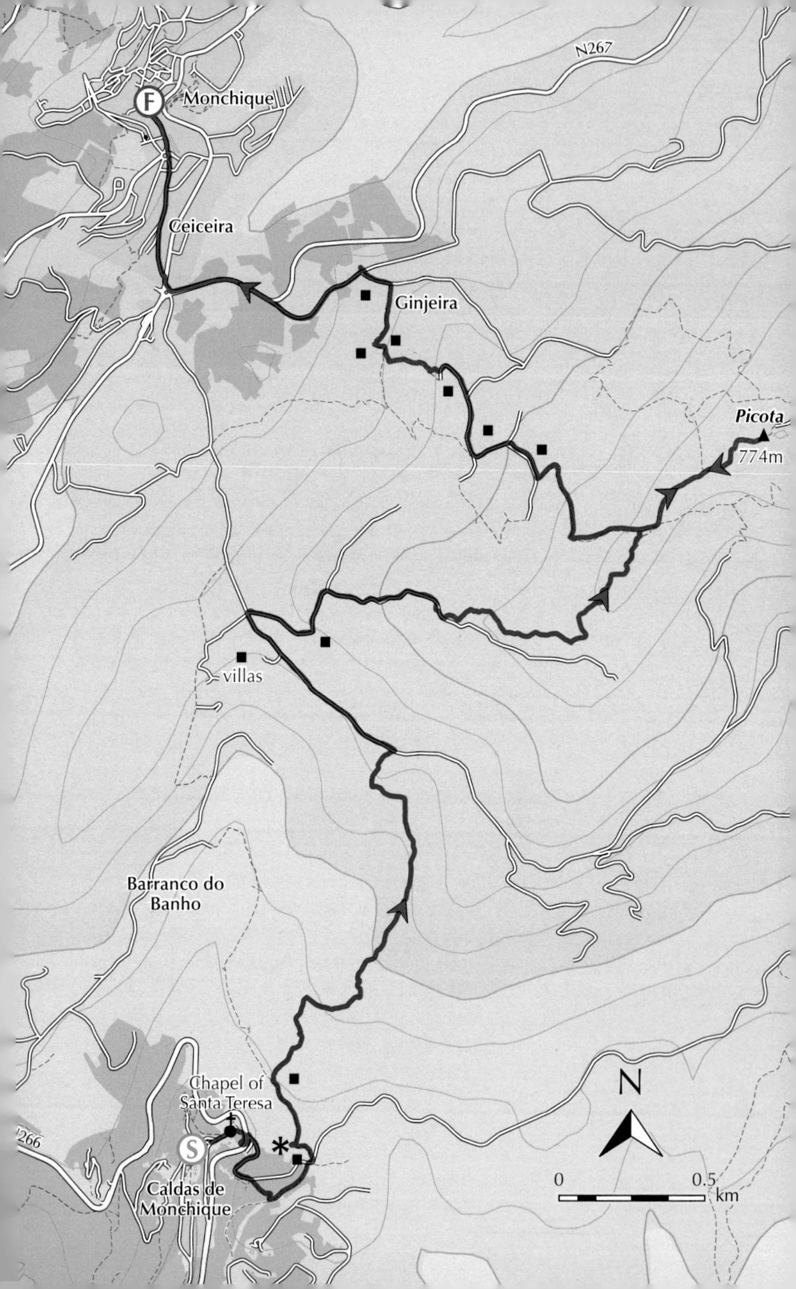

N267
Monchique
Ceiceira
Ginjeira
Picota
774m
villas
Barranco do
Banho
Chapel of
Santa Teresa
266
Caldas de
Monchique
N
0
0.5
km

In the centre of Caldas de Monchique, facing an information board, go right on the cobbled road towards the small **Chapel of Santa Teresa**.

Cross over a wooden bridge near the church; the pavement then curves around the building and continues behind it. Pass a house and then emerge onto the tarmac road; go left and a few metres later, at the bus stop, go right uphill on a cobbled road by a restaurant. Follow the small tarmac road around the building.

Leave this tarmac road to the right on the forest track marked in yellow and red.

This track is soon crossed by two others in quick succession, but continue straight on both times. Arrive at another forest track, keep right and immediately after that, go left. This is marked with a yellow/red sign. Pass two houses. After the buildings, ignore a track on the left and arrive back at the tarmac road, where you keep right. Just after the building, turn left on a wide track.

A few minutes later arrive at the *miradouro* (**viewpoint**) from where you can enjoy the first fine views. Continue along the track which bends right, with views on your left. Ignore the track on the right and continue straight on. About 250m from the *miradouro* look out for an unmarked, narrow path leading uphill between bushes on the right. This narrow, stony path firstly goes through dense vegetation, but soon views open up towards the hills scattered with houses. Ascend – often over huge rocks – with excellent views. The path is not marked but it is clearly visible and easy to follow.

There are views towards the south; the coast and Portimão are visible on a clear day.

◄ Pines and shrubs populate the hillside as you ascend over huge rocks, and soon you can spot Fóia on the left. The path might be overgrown in places; you walk over a wooden 'bridge' then cross a narrow stream and then continue to ascend on rocks again.

When a path joins from the left, keep right uphill and about 50min after joining the narrow path emerge onto a tarmac road. The narrow path continues on its other side but sadly it is now fenced off with a "Private property, no entry" sign, so go left and follow the tarmac road for about 10min, ignoring a dirt track on the right. Notice

Ascending on a narrow rocky path towards Picota

some **villas** on the left, and where a dirt track crosses the tarmac road, take the track uphill on the right hand side. Immediately after leaving the tarmac road, ignore the wide path on the left. There are some views towards the coast on the right.

Pass a house and then ignore the track on the right and continue straight on, uphill. At the junction go right, slightly uphill. Ignore the track with the 'private land' sign on the right and walk across a logged area. You will then walk through a dense section. Notice the 'Private property no entry' sign on the right (this would have been the other end of the path from the tarmac road if you were permitted to use it). Leave the track to the left on a narrow path fringed by dense vegetation, among trees (a cairn might mark this). Ignore a path joining from the left and then, when the path splits, keep left. ▶

This section has occasional red paint marks on rocks.

When the path splits again, keep right on the clearer path. It might be a bit overgrown here, but soon the peak of Picota comes into view in front of you. When the path splits again, keep left towards Picota and at the next junction bear left again. Emerge onto a dirt track and go right uphill. At a junction with signs, go left on the GR13 (Via Algarviana) as the 'Picota (550m)' sign indicates.

Ignore the track on the left with the white/red cross and ascend over rocks to the peak.

From the peak you can retrace your steps to Caldas de Monchique; this will only take you about 2hr.

There is a small look-out tower on the peak. You can enjoy a 360 degree panorama from Picota's summit (774m). There are great views towards Monchique village, and Fóia's peak with its antennas, as well as towards the coast and Portimão. ◂

There are cork oaks and moss-covered rocks by the road.

To continue to Monchique village, retrace your steps to the dirt track junction where you joined the GR13, with the 'Monchique 2.5km' sign. Go right as the sign indicates. Descend on this wide path marked with a white/red/yellow sign. Views open up towards Fóia. About 15min from the junction, pass a house, curve around the building and at the junction keep right on the surfaced road as the sign indicates. ◂ Continue to descend, and at the next intersection, keep left and pass a house. The surfaced road is signposted with white/red/yellow signs.

Soon after the house, another road joins from the left, but keep right. You have views towards the houses

of Monchique. At the next junction, bear left and stay on the road. Pass another building, and then a dirt track joins from the right. Continue straight on the surfaced road; it then bends left. This surfaced road leads towards a house; upon reaching the building, go right on a path. There is a drystone wall on the left and moss-covered rocks and cork oaks near the path as you descend. Reach a junction; the PR2 route goes left; however keep right and follow the GR13 (Via Algarviana) sign.

Soon, walk along a fence, pass a covered water reservoir, and you can enjoy the views towards Monchique and Fóia. Arrive at an asphalt road junction where you keep left downhill. Monchique is in front of you. Reach another tarmac road and keep left, ignoring any side roads. About 400m later reach the N267 road; go left. Another 400m later, arrive at a roundabout with a supermarket, from where you can walk for about another 500m to Monchique centre.

Views to Fóia and Monchique village from the top of Picota

WALK 12

Fóia–Penedo do Buraco circular

Start/finish	Car park on Fóia. Opposite the café there is an information board marking the beginning of the trail. (N37.315530, W8.592480)
Distance	7.5km
Total ascent/descent	305m
Grade	2
Time	2hr 30min
Refreshments	Snack bar on Fóia, none along the way.
Access	Monchique village is located on the N266 road, from the village you take the N266–3 road to Fóia.

This circular trail, starting from the peak of Fóia, is part of the 17km long PR5MCQ Cascades trail around Fóia's slopes. However, if you only want to do a shorter trail, you can still enjoy some fine views along this path. For those looking for a longer walk it can easily be combined with the Barbelote waterfall circular, Walk 13. It is a signposted trail; every turn-off is well marked and very easy to follow.

Start by the information board; head towards the **antennas**, and when the road splits, go left. Follow the narrow tarmac road with some great views. Leave this tarmac road to the left as the yellow/red (PR5) sign indicates. Descend on the terraced slope, passing the ruin of a house. Continue downhill towards the houses of Penedo do Buraco. In the springtime, water trickles down near the path.

Eucalyptus grows near the path.

At a junction; go right, follow the signs by some cultivated land and arrive on a small tarmac road. ◂ Pass a small house and a **picnic site** and arrive on another tarmac road where keep right as the sign indicates. Pass some houses, and when the road splits, keep left, slightly downhill. The houses of **Penedo do Buraco** are scattered on the

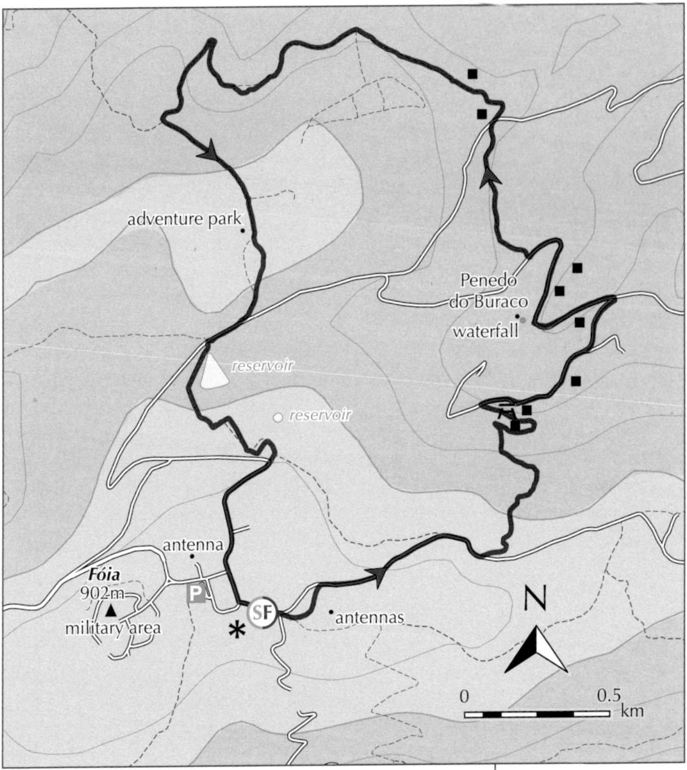

slope. At the junction, keep sharply left as the sign indicates. Continue on the tarmac road; notice a **waterfall** on the left side of the road and follow the road slightly uphill.

About an hour after leaving Fóia peak, leave the tarmac road to the right after the houses, as the sign indicates. When the dirt track splits, take the left branch, and pass the ruin of a house and an abandoned trough. As you are gently ascending, you can enjoy some views of the hills on the right hand side. Arrive at another track with a building; keep right. Ignore two tracks in quick succession on the right, and enjoy some great views.

Ascend on the stony path, and pass a house. Ignore the track on the left, carry straight on and soon more views open up to the right. Eucalyptus grows by the track. Ignore an overgrown track on the right, and carry straight on along the well-trodden track. Then ignore two tracks in quick succession on the left. Hills – criss-crossed with dirt tracks – dominate the views on the right and there are old house ruins scattered on the slope as you follow the track. Ignore a track on the right, and carry straight on as the sign indicates.

You can enjoy views towards the east and north. Hills stretch into the endless horizon.

Vegetation is slowly claiming back the terraces and abandoned ruins of houses which illustrate a place that was once inhabited and cultivated. ◄ As you ascend, pass another house lost in undergrowth overlooking the hills. (You have views to the track you came along.) Ignore the overgrown track on the right and carry straight on. Head towards the antenna on the nearby hill, on a grassy path with views on your left. Ignore an overgrown path on the left, and carry straight on as the sign indicates. At a junction, continue straight on,

An overgrown house overlooking the hills

along the fence of the **adventure park**, with Fóia in front of you. Keep left by the adventure park entrance; a few minutes later arrive back at the track and carry straight on towards Fóia with views towards the houses of Penedo do Buraco on the left. Emerge onto a tarmac road and keep right. A track leaves the tarmac road to the right; this is where you can join Walk 13. ▶

Great views from the trail as it crosses Barbelote

If you want to do the 17km trail, go right and follow Walk 13.

There is **reservoir** behind a fence on the left. The trail continues behind the fence. Go through the flap-like gate and continue alongside the reservoir, which initially runs parallel to the road. When the path splits, keep right uphill towards the antennas.

Arrive on a wide path, keep left and then right on a narrow path. Walk towards the **antennas** and curve around another **reservoir**. Go through another flap-like gate and emerge onto a tarmac road. Keep right (the Via Algarviana trail goes left) and follow the tarmac road back to the **car park** at Fóia's peak, which is only a few minutes away.

WALK 13

Barbelote waterfall circular

Start/finish	Car park on Fóia. Opposite the café there is an information board marking the beginning of the trail. (N37.315530, W8.592480)
Distance	13.5km
Total ascent/descent	610m
Grade	3
Time	4hr 30min
Refreshments	Snack bar on Fóia, none along the trail
Access	Monchique village is located on the N266 road; from the village you take the N266–3 road to Fóia.

This trail is part of the 17km long PR5MCQ Cascades trail starting from the peak of Fóia. Admire two waterfalls along the trail and then walk on the terraced slope, scattered with Barbelota's slowly decaying houses. This trail can easily be added to Walk 12; however, if you want to do the whole PR5MCQ then start with Walk 12.

From the *miradouro* (**viewpoint**) on Fóia's peak, walk along the right side of the building; follow the tarmac road, passing an **antenna** on your right. A few minutes later at a bend in the road, arrive at a fenced area. There is a flap-like gate in the fence, go through it and curve around a small **reservoir**. Go left and then keep right on a wide path. Descend towards another **reservoir** with the antennas behind you; when the path splits, keep left. Follow the narrow path parallel to the road, arrive at a flap-like gate and emerge onto the road.

Cross the tarmac road and continue left on the stony track (as the PR5 sign indicates) downhill. You might notice a building on the right, far from the track. Ignore the track on the left and carry straight on as the sign indicates. (This section of the walk is part of the Via Algarviana long-distance trail and is marked with white/red as well as yellow/

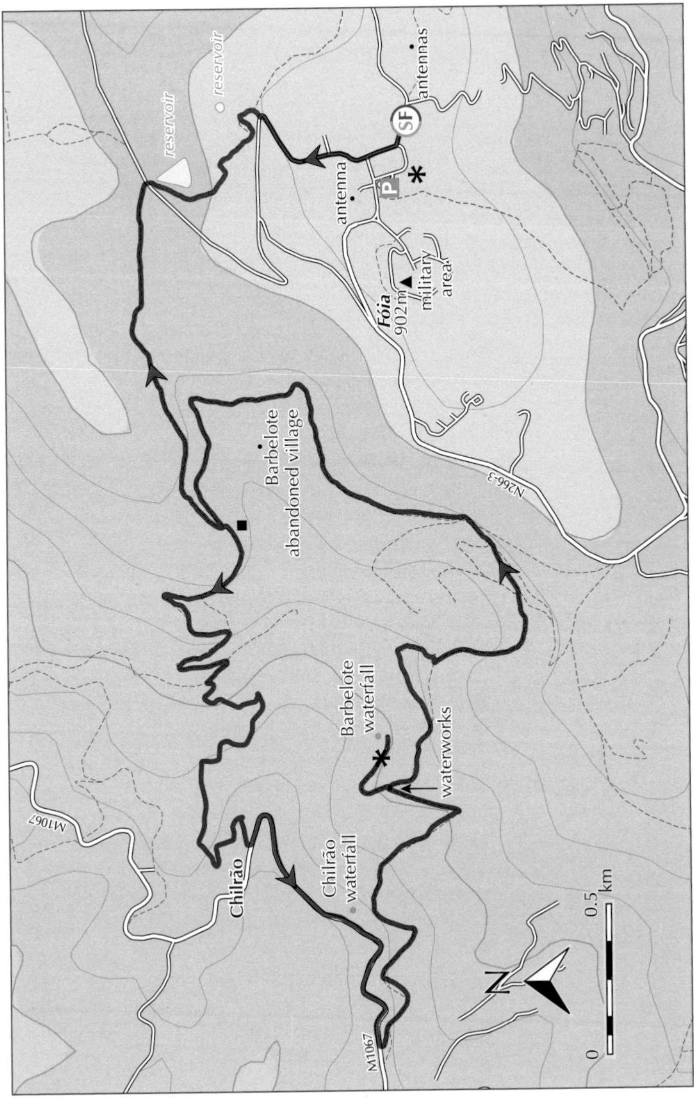
reservoir
reservoir
antennas
SF
antenna
P
Fóia
902m
military
area
Barbelote
abandoned village
N266-3
Barbelote
waterfall
waterworks
M1067
Chilrão
Chilrão
waterfall
M1067
N
0
0.5
km

red PR5 signs). Wind turbines and Fóia's peak dominate the views on the left. There is a ruin you might notice.

Ignore a track on the right and carry straight on along the well-trodden track. Soon you have views towards the terraced slope with **Barbelote's abandoned houses** on the left. Continue to descend and arrive at the junction about 20min from the tarmac road; go right (it is marked with yellow/red as PR5MCQ Percurso das Cascatas). You will return to this junction from the track on the left. ◂

Cork oak and eucalyptus grow by the track and hills fill the horizon.

Ignore any tracks and paths joining from either side and descend on the well-trodden forest track for about 50–60min. There are signs along the trail. The views are initially dominated by the once-cultivated terraced slopes with abandoned houses on the left. You then walk among trees and have some views of the hills dotted with houses on the right.

Emerge onto a tarmac road, keep left and about 10min later arrive at a **waterfall** (Cascata do Chilrão). To get closer to the waterfall, follow the slightly overgrown path on the left hand side of the road. Then continue slightly uphill on the tarmac road, with views to the right. Leave the tarmac road to the left uphill on a track soon after the Pé de Frio sign. At the dirt track junction, go left as the sign indicates and then ignore the track on the right. The track follows the contour of the mountain-side where you can enjoy the views of the slope scattered with houses and a snaking road.

Ignore a track on the left, and keep right uphill. You might hear trickling water nearby. ◂ At a junction, go left uphill on a grassy path (the forest track goes right). A few minutes later, arrive on a track and keep left (in the springtime, a rushing stream might be crossing the dirt track on the right). Walk alongside a fenced area and arrive at a junction by the **waterworks**. From here you can make a 500m (there-and-back) detour to the **waterfall** (*cascata*). Go left and follow the track to the **viewpoint**, from where you can see the waterfall. Then retrace your steps to this same junction. If you went to see the waterfall, carry straight on. (Coming from the trail without the detour to the waterfall, go right.)

There is a stream near the track.

Cascata do Barbelote is only a 500m detour

Stay on this well-trodden track slightly uphill as the sign indicates. Ignore the track on the right. You can enjoy some views towards the slope with the abandoned buildings on it and you might have another glimpse of the waterfall too. Leave this track to the left as the sign indicates by an electric pole about 5–8min after the junction with the fenced waterworks. Descend towards the abandoned houses.

Take the narrow path to the right uphill just before reaching the ruins (**Barbelote**). Ascend on this slightly overgrown path and arrive back on a track, and keep left uphill. Enjoy some more views of the once-cultivated and inhabited slopes as you pass some house ruins by

The hillside is scattered with the abandoned houses of Barbelote and you can see some of the antennas on Fóia in front of you.

the dirt track. ◀ Ignore the track on the left and stay on the dirt track. At the junction, join the Via Algarviana route, and continue straight on. At the next junction, keep left. A few minutes later, ignore the path on the right. Soon you pass a pen; in the springtime there might be trickling water by the track. Go around the valley and at the junction go right uphill (the left track is the one you took earlier). About 20min later reach a tarmac road. Cross it and the signposted trail continues alongside the reservoir behind the fence.

The abandoned settlement of Barbelote

Go through the flap-like gate and continue alongside the reservoir, which initially runs parallel to the road. When the path splits, keep right uphill towards the antennas.

Arrive on a wide path, keep left and then right on a narrow path. Walk towards the **antennas** and curve around another reservoir. Emerge onto a tarmac road through another flap-like gate. Keep right (the Via Algarviana goes left) and follow the tarmac road back to the **car park** at Fóia peak which is only a few minutes away.

WALK 14

Marmelete circular

Start/finish	Marmelete, information board in the centre, near the church (N37.309362, W8.666551)
Distance	9.5km
Total ascent/descent	330m
Grade	2
Time	3hr
Refreshments	Water is available in the village (near the playground by the bus stop), there is a Snack bar in the small centre.
Access	Marmelete village is located along the N267 road, about 19km west of Caldas de Monchique. There is a limited bus service between Monchique and Marmelete, check the timetable and seek information locally before you set off.

This trail takes you through eucalyptus and cork oak forests, and you can enjoy some great views from a small peak. There is a network of paths and tracks in the forest but the trail described is well signposted and marked PR6MCQ. Marmelete village is known for its medronho; the traditional Algarve fire water. A small museum is dedicated to the making of this strong, traditional drink.

Medronho is a strong spirit made from the fruit of the strawberry tree (*Arbutus unedo*). The tree only grows wild, and the fruit is collected by hand in the autumn, mainly in the Serra de Monchique, and in the Serra do Caldeirão. *Medronho* is produced mainly at home. The commercial version, available in supermarkets, is often sweetened with honey. The drink contains a high level of alcohol and in the rural areas of the Algarve, the farmers would start their day with a shot of *medronho* to help "wake their spirits".

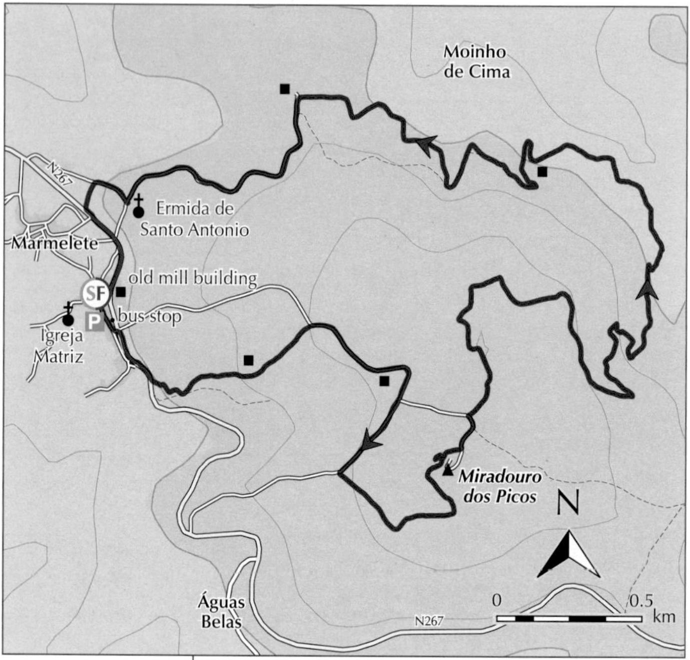

An information board marks the beginning of the PR6MCQ trail near the church. Facing the board, go left as the white/red/yellow sign indicates. This first section of the walk is part of the Via Algarviana long-distance trail, hence it is marked with white/red as well as yellow/red signs. Follow the narrow Rua Inácio V. Cabata (street), passing an **old mill building**.

Go left uphill as signposted and arrive at a tarmac road. The trail continues on the other side of the road, but returns to it a few metres further up; alternatively you can go right on this tarmac road, and then look out for a path on the left hand side. Leave the tarmac road to the left uphill, on the second yellow/red marked path (the first marked path would return to the tarmac road if you followed the signs from the village).

When it splits, carry straight on uphill, and look out for signs on your right. Emerge onto a forest track and keep left. When this track splits, take the left branch uphill. At the next split, keep right as the sign indicates. Ignore the track on the left, carry straight on, and pass a building. ▶ Ignore an overgrown track on the left, then one on the right, and stay on the signposted track. Reach a narrow tarmac road, keep right and follow it as the white/red/yellow sign indicates.

Pass two buildings and stay on the narrow tarmac road. Ignore a track on the left, and at the next junction with signs, keep slightly right as the PR6 Marmelete yellow/red sign indicates (the Via Algarviana route goes left).

Then ignore a track on the left and a few minutes later, just before reaching the ruin of a stone house, leave

Great views from the top of Miradouro dos Picos

Cork oaks populate the hillside.

the narrow tarmac road to the left. Follow this forest track through eucalyptus forest for about 8–10min, and then leave it on a narrow signposted path to the left. Ascend on the narrow path to the peak (**Miradouro dos Picos**). Unfortunately, there is an antenna on the top, but you can still enjoy some great views towards the coast and towards the antenna-dotted Fóia.

From the peak descend along the fence, and emerge onto a tarmac road by a gate. Follow the road downhill, and at a junction keep left on the narrow tarmac road as the yellow/red sign indicates (the Via Algarviana goes to the right).

About 50m from this junction, leave the tarmac road to the right on the first forest track, as the yellow/red sign indicates. Follow this forest track through eucalyptus forest. There are some boulders near the track. Ignore any paths joining from either side, and stay on the forest track as the yellow/red signs indicate. Arrive at a track junction, keep right and immediately ignore a track on the left, and carry straight on. The track narrows down to a path for a while and then widens back to a forest track again. As you follow the eucalyptus-lined track you have a glimpse of Fóia in the distance.

At the junction, go right as the sign indicates and a few minutes later at the next junction, bear right again. Ignore the narrow paths on both sides of the track, and stay on the forest track. (These narrow paths starting from the forest track, are most probably used by mountain bikers). At the junction, go left slightly downhill through eucalyptus forest. ◂ Pass a ramshackle building and keep right downhill. Cork oak populate the hillside alongside the path. Ignore a narrow path going steeply downhill on the left. Descend with views to eucalyptus, cork and pine covered slopes. Ignore a narrow path on the right, and stay on the forest track. There is a small ravine on your right. You might hear trickling water. Ignore a track on the left, follow the forest track bending right, pass some ruins and then keep left downhill as the sign indicates. Ignore two paths on the right and carry straight on. Immediately after the second joining path, keep right downhill on a narrow path

Enjoy some views towards Fóia on your right. You might spot some buildings on the slope.

beneath cork oaks. ▶ Ignore a trail joining from the left, continue straight on, and then keep left at a track junction.

There are some beehives along the path; take care!

Follow the forest track slightly downhill with some views to the nearby slopes. Pass an overgrown ruin and ignore a path on the left. There are some houses along the track. Walk along a big building with views on the left. As you ascend, ignore the track on left. And then continue slightly downhill. Arrive on a dirt track, keep left as the sign indicates. Leave the track to the right, downhill on a marked path. You can enjoy some views towards Fóia.

Join a dirt track in a road bend and follow it uphill. At the dirt track junction with a building, go left, and keep right by the next house. Ignore a track joining from the right, carry straight on. As you approach Marmelete, there are more and more houses along the track. Ignore tracks on both sides and head towards the chapel by the road. Arrive at **Ermida de Santo Antonio chapel**, go right, and before reaching a group of houses, keep left on a pavement along the field. Arrive on the main road, keep left and walk back to the village centre which is only a few minutes away. If you follow the yellow/red signs, the trail takes you through the narrow streets of the village before returning to the starting point.

The bark of the cork oak can only be harvested every nine years

WALK 15

Barragem da Bravura

Start/finish	Barragem da Bravura (N37.200961, W8.699128)
Distance	7.5km
Total ascent/descent	160m
Grade	1
Time	2hr 15min
Refreshments	There is a small restaurant near the dam at the beginning of the trail. Opening hours: Wednesday-Sunday 11:00–17:00, Monday and Tuesday closed.
Access	No public transport to the reservoir. From the N125 road, at Odiáxere take the N125–9 to the Baragem de Bravura. There are plenty of places to park by the restaurant building.

The dam was built in the late 1950s to provide irrigation for the south-western Algarve. Being only about 25km from Lagos, this peaceful place is great for leisure walking. There are maps of some short walks around the reservoir available from the small restaurant at the beginning of the trail. You can enjoy some great views of the reservoir surrounded by rolling hills, as you follow this trail.

Eucalyptus grows alongside the path.

From the **car park** follow the signs: 'dam wall' around the **restaurant building**. Descend some stairs towards the **dam** behind the building and walk across the wall; keep left on the narrow path along the shore. ◂ Ignore the path on the right and curve around one of the many tongues of the reservoir. Walk through eucalyptus forest; at a small junction carry straight on with the reservoir on your left, and soon at the next junction keep left. About 15min later, ignore a path joining from the right and continue alongside the reservoir.

As you curve around the lake you can see the dam wall and the building at the start of the trail.

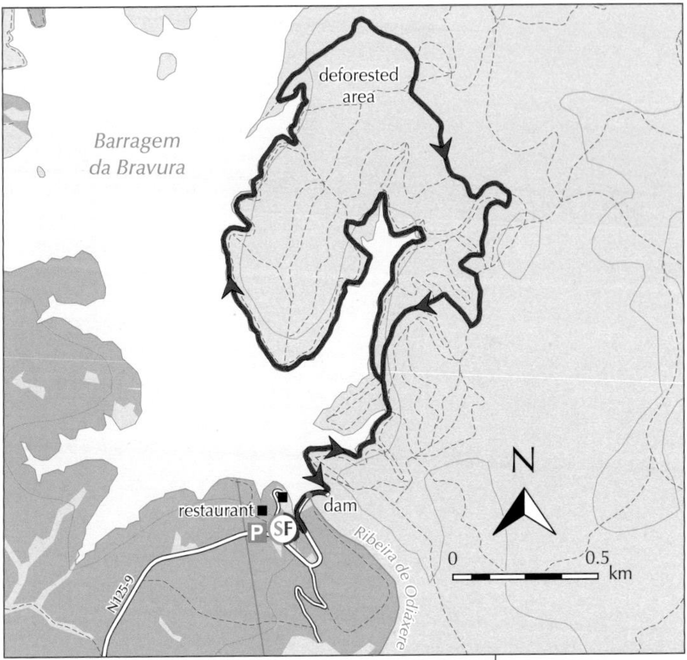

A narrow path leads down to Barragem da Bravura

Ignore another path going uphill on the right and carry straight on alongside the reservoir. Ignore the next path on the right, and a few minutes later the path turns away from the reservoir, slightly uphill. When it splits, keep left. You can enjoy some views of the reservoir surrounded by rolling hills. ◂

There is a network of paths and your route is unmarked.

At the junction, keep right (the reservoir is on your right) and then at the next intersection, keep left downhill; the other branch goes back towards the water. Follow the path and enjoy the fine views of the rolling hills. Ignore two consecutive tracks on the right. Then keep right at the next junction. When the path splits, keep left downhill and a few minutes later reach a junction; keep left and almost immediately go left again and retrace your steps along the reservoir's shore.

The trail goes through eucalyptus forest

WALK 16

Barão de São João art trail

Start/finish	Barão de São João, opposite the Cultural Centre (N37.139521, W8.779706)
Distance	7km
Total ascent/descent	155m
Grade	1
Time	2hr
Refreshments	Café/bar in Barão de São João, water available at the picnic site.
Access	Barão de São João is located on the M535 road 5km south-west of Bensafrim, there are plenty of places to park near the Cultural Centre. Some buses serve the village from Lagos. See [[]]Appendix C[[]] for transport information.

You can choose from two circular walks following the contour of the forested mountainside starting from Barão de São João. This shorter route is waymarked as (PR1LGS) PR Pedra do Galo 6,1 km, and yellow/red signs are used along the trail. In springtime the lush forest is home to several different species of orchid.

Barão de São João and the surrounding area are popular with artistic expats, and many foreigners live in the village. You can see plenty of **art** in the village; and also look out for some rock carvings in the forest, made by a local artist.

There is an information board located almost opposite the **Cultural Centre**. Facing the information board, start left uphill on the tarmac road.

The road becomes a wide dirt track as you walk slightly uphill. Shortly after the start, ignore a track on the right and carry straight on, as the sign indicates. At

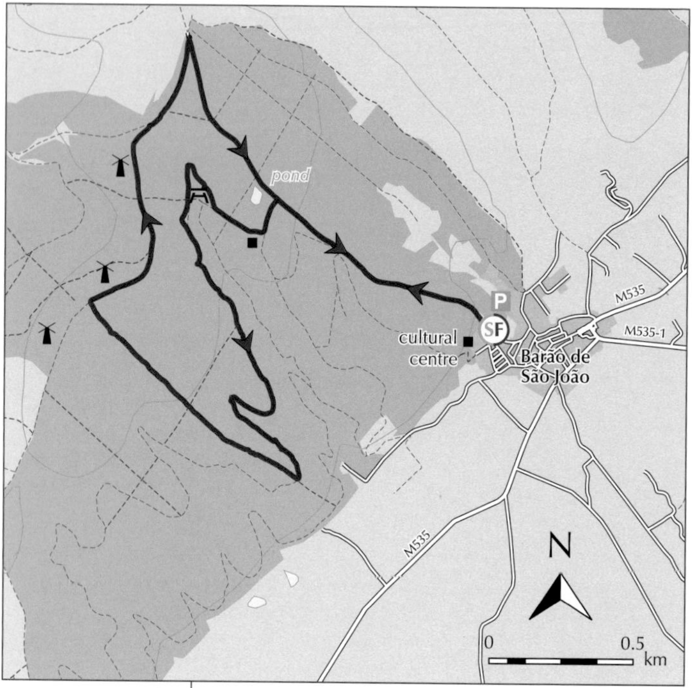

a junction, carry straight on (ignoring two tracks on the left) and a few minutes later at the next junction there is a sign: Circuito de Mantecão, Parque de Merendas; keep left. You can see wind turbines nearby.

Reach a **building**, keep right by its walls and arrive at a parking/camping area. There is a toilet building by the path, then reach a large **picnic site**. There is running water, a playground, plenty of picnic tables and benches and a barbecue area here. Walk around the picnic area, following the PR1 route sign.

The forest sounds are accompanied by the constant swish from the wind turbines.

Mediterranean Pine (pinus pinea) grows by the forest track. Ignore the track on the right, and stay on the forest track marked with a yellow/red sign. ◂ In springtime, you might notice a tiny stream on the left and you

The track goes through pine forest

can look out for orchids by the track. Ignore the track on the right, and continue on the forest track as the sign indicates. Look out for the rock carvings by the track; some have lettering on them, others feature pictures.

About 10min after the picnic site, there are two benches by the forest track and some views of the green canopy on the left; you can almost always see a wind turbine as well. As the forest track follows the contour of the mountainside, you have some views towards Barão de São João village on the left. At the junction, go right (signposted), slightly uphill. Shrubs and pines grow by the forest track. Ignore any overgrown tracks on the left and right, and carry straight on as the yellow/red sign indicates.

A carved rock in the middle of a shallow watering hole

About 40–45min after the picnic site, notice a watering hole with a fish rock carving on the left hand side of the track. At the junction, carry straight on as the yellow/red sign indicates. There is another watering hole on the left, and then the forest track passes between two **wind turbines**. Emerge onto a wide dirt track and keep right. Follow this wide track by the wind turbines. Ignore any tracks on the left or right, and carry straight on on the wide track. At the junction – where the left hand track goes towards Vinha Velha as the GR13 route – carry straight on. When the track splits again, carry straight on, and at the next intersection the trail continues to the right. Carry straight on at the next two intersections, and arrive at the junction where you went right towards the picnic site about 30min after joining the dirt track by the wind turbines. Keep straight on and retrace your steps to the **Cultural Centre**.

WALK 17

Barão de São João forest circular

Start/finish	Barão de São João, opposite the Cultural Centre (N37.139521, W8.779706)
Distance	10km
Total ascent/descent	275m
Grade	2
Time	3hr
Refreshments	Café/bar in Barão de São João, water available at the picnic site.
Access	Barão de São João is located on the M535 road 5km south-west of Bensafrim, there are plenty of places to park near the Cultural Centre. Some buses serve the village from Lagos. See [[]]Appendix C[[]] for transport information.

This second, longer circular walk from Barão de São João takes you through lush forest, where in springtime you can look out for orchids. The first part of the trail briefly follows a section of the GR13; after that the trail detailed here is not signposted, but the tracks follow the contour of the mountainside, with some fine views along the way. The picnic site towards the end of the walk is a great place to stop for a rest before returning to the village.

There is an information board located almost opposite the Cultural Centre. Facing the board, start left uphill on the tarmac road.

The road becomes a wide dirt track as you walk slightly uphill. Shortly after the start, ignore a track on the right and carry straight on, as the sign indicates. At a junction, carry straight on (ignoring two tracks on the left) and a few minutes later at the next junction there is a sign: Circuito de Mantecão, Parque de Merendas; carry straight on (you will be returning to this junction from the track on the left).

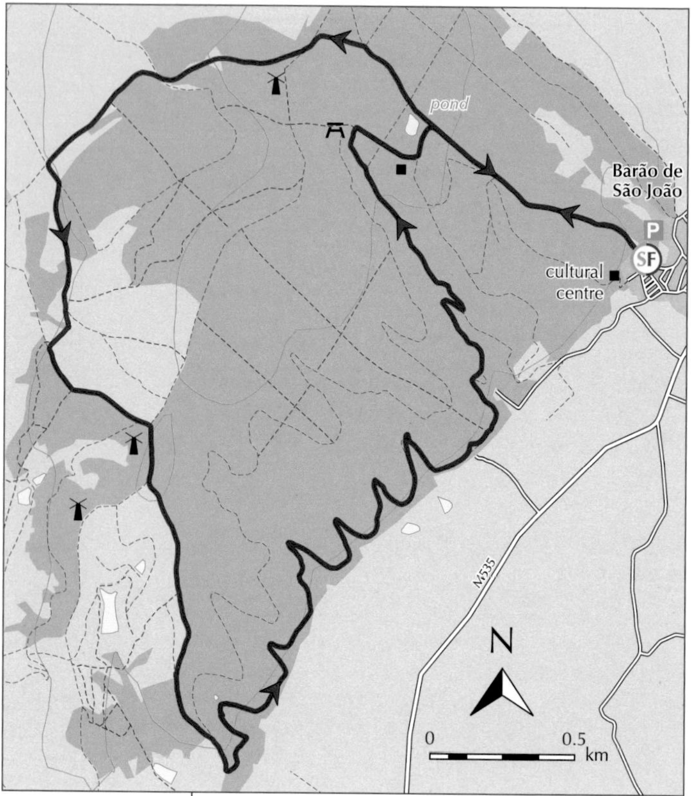

Ignore tracks on either side and carry straight on, and at the three-way junction, go left towards Vinha Velha. A few minutes later, at the next intersection, keep left again and then, when the track splits, keep right towards Vinha Velha, as the GR13 sign indicates. Follow the track slightly downhill. There is some thorny gorse by the track. At the junction (about 15min after leaving the yellow/red marked trail,) carry straight on as the GR13 red/white sign indicates (the right hand track is private (*privado*)). You can spot some cork oaks near the track.

Forest track near Barão de São João

At the clearing, before reaching Vinha Velha, there are some minor tracks marked with a cross on either side of the wide track. The GR13 trail continues straight on; however, go left on the small forest track marked with a cross. A few minutes later, notice a tiny reservoir on the left, and after the reservoir, keep slightly to the right. ▸ As you follow the shrub-lined, undulating forest track, ignore a path joining on the left and continue straight on.

Hills with wind turbines dominate the views on the right.

There are some views towards the buildings of Vinha Velha on the right. Ignore an overgrown track on the right, and stay on the slightly undulating forest track. Views open up to tree tops and wind turbines. Walk past a **wind turbine** and at a major track junction (about 30min after joining the unmarked forest track before Vinha Velha) go right. A few minutes later, when the track splits, keep left. Ignore two paths on the left and then one on the right and carry straight on. ▸

There are views to the south; you can spot Barão de São Miguel village on a hilltop.

Eucalyptus and pine populate this area. At the dirt track junction, carry straight on slightly downhill. Ignore the track on the right, then keep sharply left when the track splits. The track follows the contour of the hillside and you can see some farms on the right near the forest track. Ignore a track joining from the right, keep left on the wider track, then ignore a track on the left and carry straight on.

About 10min later at the junction, go left uphill, and a few minutes later ignore a track on the left and carry straight on. Arrive at a **picnic area**. Join the PR1 route next to the picnic site, and keep right, and then left by a **building**. Arriving at the junction with signs, go right and retrace your steps back to the **Cultural Centre**.

Wind turbines tower over the canopy of the forest

SOUTH COAST

Views back towards Praia do Vau (Walk 22)

SOUTH COAST

Views towards Lagos (Walk 24)

The South Coast includes bustling coastal towns with several holiday resorts and small fishing villages which have grown into tourist resorts. The summer months see thousands of people on the rock-lined sandy beaches and the coast throbs with life. However, walking is the best way to explore the coastline. Sea stacks, almost vertical cliffs and sinkholes dominate the views on the coastal path. There are ruins of forts and lighthouses along the trails. And there are plenty of restaurants to stop at for fresh sea food. The coastal walks can be extended to a longer day by walking two sections. It is also possible to tackle the coastal path (Walks 24–27) as a three or four-day trek. Tourists are well catered for in the coastal towns with a wide range of accommodation, but it is recommended to book ahead. **Lagos** or **Luz** with its beautiful beaches, restaurants and shops can be a great base for coastal walks. Those wanting larger, more vibrant towns with big hotels should consider **Albufeira** or **Portimão**. Walking along the coast is best done outside the hot summer months.

Note that with most of the coastal walks, the route can easily be altered via the network of paths running along several sections of the coast, so the distance and time can vary slightly accordingly.

WARNING

On every section of the coastal path, take extra care and don't get too close to the edge. This is an ever-changing environment, the land is constantly eroding away; therefore the routes might alter from one year to the next.

WALK 18

Albufeira to Galé

Start	Rua Marina de Albufeira near the Marina in Albufeira (N37.085257, W8.269448)
Finish	Galé
Distance	8.5 km
Total ascent	125m
Total descent	145m
Grade	2
Time	2hr 30min–3hr
Refreshments	Plenty in Albufeira. There are some small cafés/bars operating throughout the season (May to Oct) at the beaches along the way. But do take plenty of water, especially if it is a hot day, as there is no shade on the route. Beach bar/restaurant: Praia dos Arrifes, Praia São Rafael, Praia da Coelha, Praia do Castelo, Praia do Manuel Lourenço.
Access	If you are arriving in Albufeira by bus, bear in mind that the bus terminal is about 1.5km outside town. You can take a local bus towards the marina or there are taxis at the terminal.
Warning	Take care on the cliff-tops and don't get too close to the edge. Note that due to constant erosion, the trail may change from one year to the next.

A network of footpaths criss-crosses the dramatic coast. Vertical cliffs adjoin small sandy beaches, and the air is often filled with the smell of salty sea water. Listen to the waves crashing onto the rocks and as the path runs close to the edge you can admire some fascinating rock formations. You might want to look for fossils or soak up the views. There are opportunities to stop for a swim at one of the beaches along the way, so maybe pack swimming gear.

The trail described is linear; however, it is possible to retrace your steps. While it is not a long-distance route, you might want to take your time, so the outward journey will take a lot longer. If retracing your steps to Albufeira you most probably won't follow the cliffs so strictly and will cut off some outcrops, meaning you can get back significantly faster. Alternatively, if you are planning to take a bus from Galé, check the timetable locally before you set off.

From the **marina**, follow the Alamedada Orada road, reach Rua Marina de Albufeira and keep left uphill. When you reach a junction, turn sharply right to Caminho da Balleira; soon it becomes a dirt track. About 200m from the junction, leave the dirt track to the left towards the ocean. If you are driving, you can park along this dirt track.

There are several paths; for the best views, try to choose a path closer to the cliff edge, but at a safe distance from the drop. You will be following the contour of the coast with the ocean on your left. The path often splits

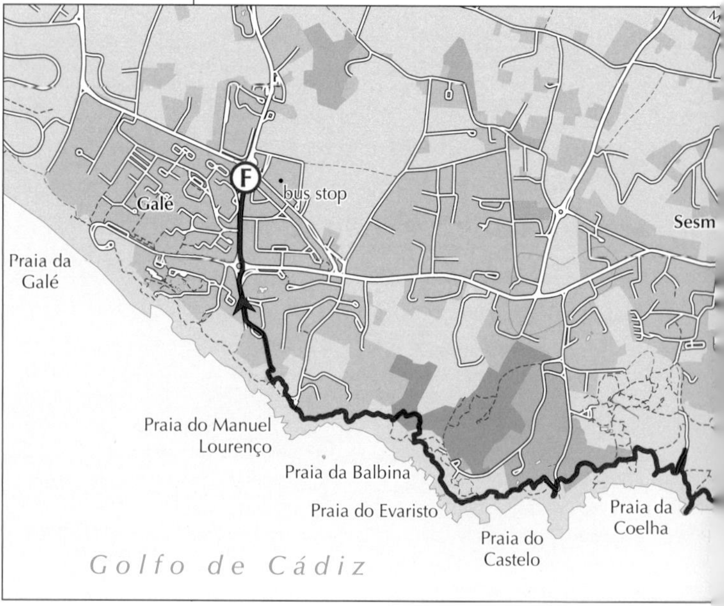

and then rejoins, so most of the time it doesn't really matter which branch you take. ▶ There are interesting rock formations to look out for. Walk between small shrubs and very soon you can enjoy views towards the first small beach, surrounded by rocks. Arrive at **Praia dos Arrifes** (beach) car park about 20–30min after joining the coastal path. This is the first beach and the first opportunity to stop for a swim along the way. The snack bar at the beach is open during beach season (mid-May to mid-Oct).

Take care on the constantly eroding cliffs!

Walk across the car park. There are villas on your right and a longer sandy beach appears after the car park. The path then continues after the parking area. It curves around the beach with the ocean on your left. Climb the wooden steps and continue on a boardwalk. When the boardwalk splits, go right and about 30min after Praia dos Arrifes arrive at the next car park and **Praia de São Rafael**. There is a small restaurant here for further refreshments.

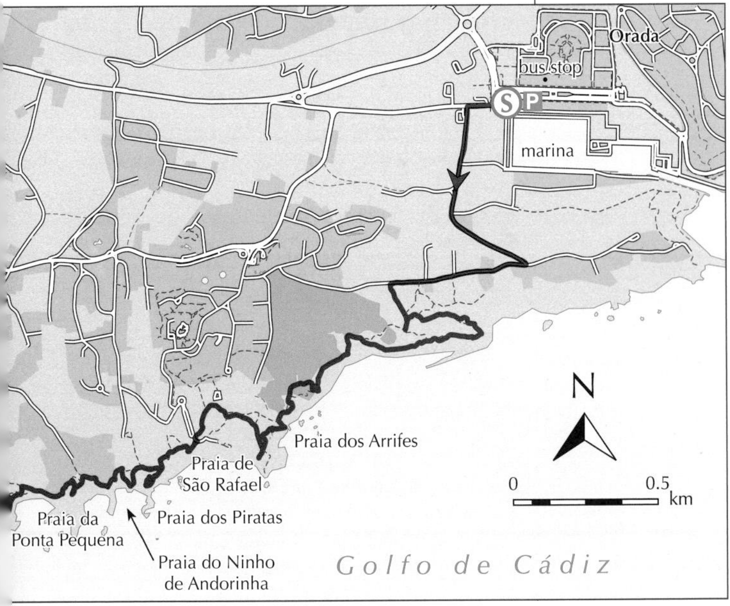

Rocky coastline soon after Praia de São Rafael

Walk across the car park; you might notice red-painted circles on rocks (this marking indicates the coastal path further on as well). Walk slightly uphill by the fence and then continue closer to the cliff.

After the beach, look out for some really big, deep sinkholes. Take care and don't walk or stand on the edge. Keep the sinkholes on your left and continue along the fence. At the end of the fence keep straight on, descend slightly and then continue along the fence again.

You get closer to the cliff and then follow some eroded stone steps. More rocks with painted red circle markings can be spotted along the way and are a great indicator that you are on the right path. The path is lined with bushes and a short section might be a bit overgrown. Pass a villa and notice some houses on the right. When you see a guard rail on the right hand side, go towards it, and then continue along it. A group of white houses can be seen on the right. ◂ Soon the coastline stretches out in front of you as you keep closer to the edge again. About

Look out for fossils in the rocks.

an hour after Praia São Rafael, another beach with rocks behind it comes into sight, and from an outcrop you can enjoy great views to the beach.

Reach a walkway and keep on towards the beach (**Praia da Coelha**). Pass a restaurant building, climb the wooden steps and then some rocks. There are more painted red spots on rocks here. There are some railings here as you walk parallel to the cliff and the ocean, with villas on your right. Follow the path along a fence. There is a small beach down on your left and soon you arrive at the car park of **Praia do Castelo** (there is also a snack bar here). From this car park, follow the road and then the path continues. Walk along the fence, keeping very close to it and pass another small beach. ▶ About 20min after leaving Praia do Castelo, arrive at **Praia do Evaristo** (beach) and then continue after its car park. Walk along the fence again, then get closer to the ocean. There is a villa on the right hand side and you pass a small beach on your left. You might have to go through a reed tunnel

There are red circle marks indicating the coastal path.

Fossilised seashells in plain sight

with a fence on your right. Cross over a small fragile wooden bridge and in the distance you can see Armação de Pêra. Soon arrive at **Praia do Manuel Lourenço** with its restaurant/bar.

You might want to stop for a swim and then retrace your steps to Albufeira or continue on the dirt track after the car park. 100m later, arrive at another car park and continue right on the tarmac road; at the junction/roundabout go straight to the centre of Galé or right to the nearest bus stop.

WALK 19

Praia do Vale do Olival to Praia da Marinha

Start	Praia do Vale do Olival (N37.102881, W8.369705)
Finish	Praia da Marinha
Distance	9.5km
Total ascent	145m
Total descent	135m
Grade	2
Time	3hr–3hr 30min, but if you want to retrace your steps from Praia da Marinha to Praia do Vale do Olival, it only takes about 1hr 30min. Allow some extra time to stop at Praia da Marinha, you may want to go for a swim if it is a warm day.
Refreshments	There are cafés and restaurants at Vale do Olival, at the beginning of the trail. There are some small cafés/bars operating throughout the season (May to October) at the beaches, but take plenty of water, especially if it is a hot day as there is no shade on the route. Beach bar/restaurant: Praia de Albandeira and Praia da Marinha.
Access	Praia do Vale do Olival is located on the M530–1 and Avenida Beira Mar road junction. There is a big car park there. If you are planning to use public transport, be aware that there are only two buses daily, on weekdays from Lagoa to Marinha beach and back. Seek information at the local tourist office. It is possible to take a taxi from Praia da Marinha at the end of your walk, but make plans before you set off.
Warning	Take care on the cliff-tops and don't get too close to the edge. Note that due to constant erosion, the trail may change from one year to the next.

This is another great coast walk, where you can admire striking rock formations and stop for a swim on small, cliff-lined beaches along the way. On this section of the coastline, you will see much evidence of erosion. The cliffs are constantly battered by the sea, and with the help of rainwater, huge sinkholes are created along the coast.

The trail described is linear; however it is possible to retrace your steps. On the return, you most probably won't follow the cliffs so strictly and can cut off some outcrops; therefore you can get back to Praia do Vale do Olival significantly faster.

This section of the coastal path can be extended to a longer day walk by continuing to Praia Vale de Centeanes (Walk 20). If you are planning to spend the night near Praia Vale de Centeanes, it is advisable to book accommodation in advance.

The trail starts at the west end of the long sandy **Vale do Olival** beach. From the car park, take the stony path by the river with the restaurant building on your left. Cross the wooden bridge and continue on the path. Just before you reach the sandy beach, keep right uphill on steps near a building. The ocean is on your left, and there is a fence and some buildings on your right. Immediately you have some great views towards the long sandy beach and rock formations. As you follow the path, notice a small beach down below and a hotel garden on your right.

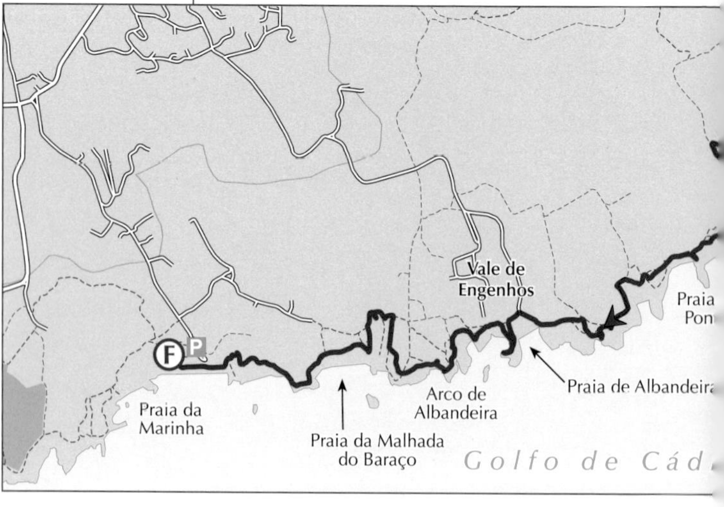

Look out for a small path among bushes on the right, just after the hotel.

Follow this path which soon becomes concreted and emerges onto a road. Keep left on the paved road. There is a hotel building on your right and the road is lined with pines. Pass the gate of the Villa vita Parc and turn left on the first available street. Take the next street on the left. Carry straight on downhill by the Pestana Viking Hotel. Then follow the cobbled path with railings, with the beach on your left. Go down some steps and then keep right uphill. Turn left by a bar building with a boat in front of it. Head towards the white church on the cliff. Walk to the **Nossa Senhora da Rocha (Our Lady of the Rock) chapel**.

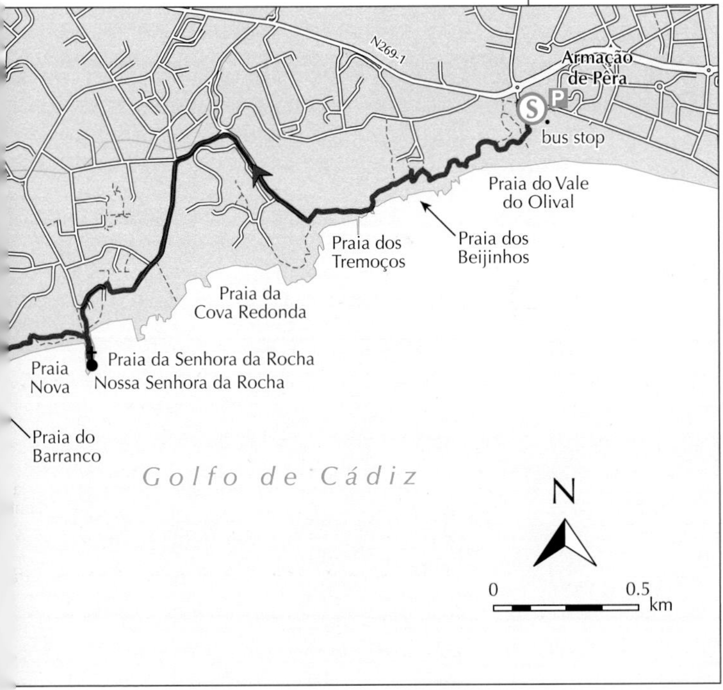

It is believed, that there was a **fort** at the time of the Arab invasion, where the **church** is today. By 1821 the fort was in ruins. Today the small white chapel located on the rock is a popular place for weddings.

From the church, retrace your steps to the coastal path and continue westwards. Notice the steep steps leading down to **Praia Nova** (Nova Beach), it is the first opportunity to stop for a swim. If that doesn't appeal, carry straight on. You might notice some red spots on some rocks, these can help you to stay on the coastal path.

The western end of Praia do Vale do Olival

Some of the huge, deep sinkholes are fenced off with wooden railings, but take care as railings are missing in places and not all sinkholes are enclosed!

A few minutes after passing the steep steps, notice a small path going left downhill, but take the path on the right as the red spot indicates. This takes you slightly inland with a small ravine on your left. When the path splits, keep left and arrive at a parking area and a dirt track. Keep left and walk towards the beach. Before your reach the sand, keep right uphill on a rocky path. Ignore the path on the right, and keep slightly left uphill with the ocean on your left. When the path splits, go left. You have views back towards the chapel. There is a network of paths running in this area, try and keep closer to the ocean but take extra care near the edge. Clusters of juniper grow in this area. ◄

Soon there is another small beach down below. There is a striking stack in the sea, resembling a giant boat. Pass another small beach down below and follow the red spots on rocks. There are more sinkholes closer to the cliff edge; you can hear as the water washes underneath the rocks. Unfortunately the information boards here have faded badly due to the strong sunshine and it is impossible to read them. Take the wide path closer to

Views of Praia de Albandeira

the cliff edge with a villa on your right and about an hour after leaving Nossa Senhora da Rocha, arrive at the car park of the **Praia de Albandeira**. There are picnic tables and a restaurant here.

Walk across the car park and the path continues. Keep left for great views, soon you will see a natural arch (**Arco de Albandeira**). There are huge sinkholes with some wooden railings and blank information boards. These sinkholes are the reminders how the coast is constantly changing. The path is occasionally marked with red spots. The path, lined with junipers, bends inland and runs parallel to a ravine. Reach a dirt track, go left downhill (a red arrow marks this). When the wide path splits, keep right as indicated; the left branch goes to the beach. When it splits again, bear left. You will see a hidden beach, which is only accessible by boat. Walk along a fence and reach the steps leading down to **Praia da Marinha**, one of the most celebrated beaches in the Algarve. Striking cliffs and good quality water make it a popular location. There is a small restaurant at the bottom of the stairs. ▶

If you want to retrace your steps, you can get back to Praia do Vale do Olival in about 1hr 30min.

WALK 20

Praia da Marinha to Praia Vale de Centeanes

Start	Praia da Marinha (N37.090179, W8.412828)
Finish	Praia Vale de Centeanes
Distance	7km
Total ascent	180m
Total descent	170m
Grade	2
Time	2hr 30min
Refreshments	Restaurants at Marinha beach, Benagil beach and Vale de Centeanes beach. Note that many of the beach cafés/restaurants are only open during the season, usually from May to October.
Access	From the N125 road take the M1154 road. From the M1154 take Estr. da Marinha to Praia da Marinha. There is a big car park at Marinha beach. Please note, if you are planning to use public transport, there are only two buses daily, on weekdays only from Lagoa to Marinha beach and back. Ask for information in tourist offices. It is possible to take a taxi to and from Praia da Marinha, but make plans before you set off for the walk.
Warning	Take care on the cliff-tops and don't get too close to the edge. Note that due to constant erosion, the trail may change from one year to the next.

This section of the coast walk is known as the Seven hanging valley trail, marked PR1LGA. It is a popular, well-trodden and signposted section of the coastal path. On this trail you can enjoy fine views of the turquoise water-washed coast. You can peer down to sinkholes and marvel at small sandy beaches surrounded by rocks.

The trail described is linear; however it is possible to retrace your steps. On the return, you most probably won't follow the cliffs so strictly and can cut off some outcrops; therefore you can get back to Praia da Marinha significantly faster.

This section of the coastal path can be extended to a full-day walk by continuing to Ferragudo (Walk 21). If you are planning to spend the night near Ferragudo it is advisable to book accommodation in advance.

Leave the **car park** by the picnic tables (west side of car park) and descend on steps by the information board. Follow the path lined with wooden railings to a viewpoint, from where you can admire rock formations. The trail is marked with yellow/red signs. Walk across a dusty parking area and follow the signs with the ocean on your left. If you look back, you have great views of Marinha beach. ▸

Rock arches, coves, stacks and sinkholes – formed by the combined work of rainwater, erosion and the sea – characterise the coastline.

As you walk by sinkholes, you can hear as the water washes below, and then admire a rock arch. Follow the signs on the rocky path and in front of you the views are dominated by the dramatic coastline.

There is a wooden railing along the trail and you have views to a small beach which is accessible only by boat. Continue along the railing and after about 45min stroll you can peek down to **Grutas de Benagil** (Benagil cave). Hear the crashing waves from below and as you look down you might see some people peering up from the bottom. They will have got there by boat. If you wish to copy them, boat trips can be booked in many places along the coast.

As you continue, **Praia de Benagil** comes into sight. Follow the yellow/red signs on the wide path which then narrows and runs between houses and a fence. Descend on steps, and arrive at a tarmac road, by the Algar restaurant building. Go left downhill. You get close to Benagil beach, where boat trips set off to see the coves and sea caves along the coast. (This is also an opportunity to stop for a swim.)

Benagil was a small fishing village until the late 20th century. Since then, tourism has played an increasingly important role. Plenty of boats still depart each day from the small rock-bordered beach, not for fishing, but to take visitors to Benagil cave and to admire the coast from the ocean.

Beautiful arches near Praia da Marinha

Continue uphill to the right on the tarmac road, away from the beach. A few metres later, leave the road to the left on some steps. Walk across the terrace of the Casa Lang restaurant and continue along houses with views to the beach. Leave the stairs to the left, on the path as the yellow/red sign indicates.

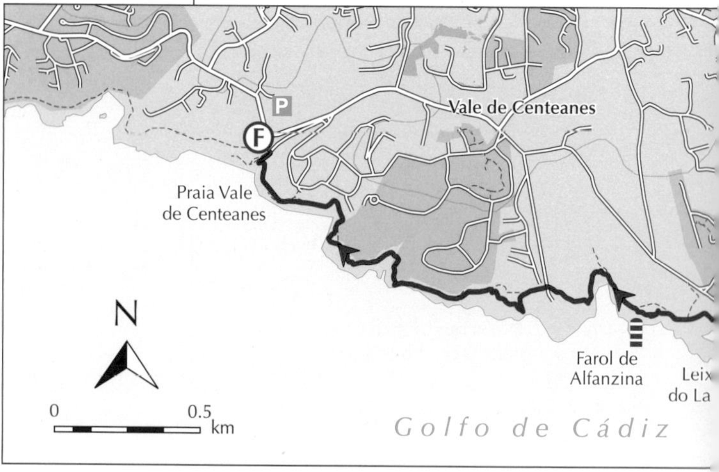

Soon, leave the buildings behind and continue closer to the edge. Enjoy some views to another small, rock-surrounded beach with a sea stack close to the shore. Arrive at **Praia do Carvalho** (Carvalho beach) car park about 25min after leaving Praia de Benagil. You can access this beach via a tunnel that starts near the information board. Climb the stairs and leave it on a narrow path to the left. Follow a shrub-lined path and admire the coastline.

▸ You can observe the power of the elements along the coast, as there are many places where the water has visibly washed under the cliffs. Soon, a lighthouse appears on the horizon. About 25min after Praia do Carvalho, pass a picnic area on a platform near the **Leixão do Ladrão** (Ladrão stack). Boats often go through this natural tunnel. Notice some villas on the right. Follow the yellow/red signs along the cliffs towards the lighthouse. Pass a huge sinkhole, you can hear the sound of water rushing underneath.

There are some information boards along this section of the trail.

Continue along the coast, past further sinkholes and arrive at **Farol de Alfanzina** (lighthouse) about 50min after leaving Praia do Carvalho.

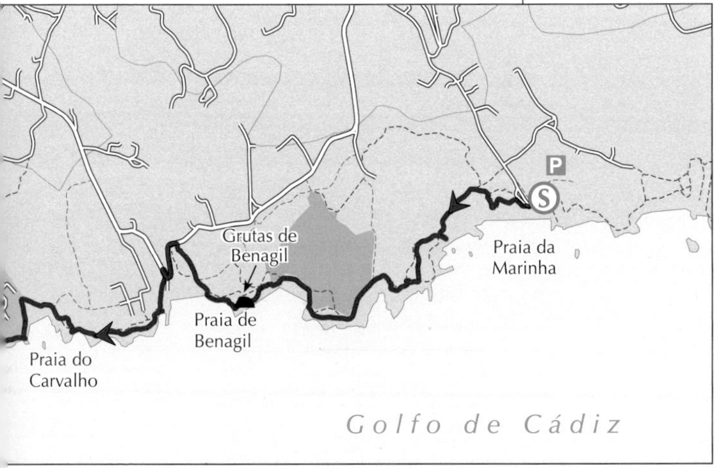

Farol de Alfanzina (lighthouse)

Farol de Alfanzina lighthouse – located between the Cape St Vincent lighthouse and the Santa Maria lighthouse – was built in 1919 and from 1920 helped boats and ships to navigate. The lights can be seen from 30 miles away.

The views are dominated by the jagged coastline and vertical cliffs.

Cross the tarmac road in front of the lighthouse. There is a car park on the right, continue straight on along the fence. There are houses on the right and notice a huge sinkhole on the left, just after the lighthouse. Then walk along a railing, follow the signs and soon pass a small picnic area. Shortly you come to another sinkhole with an information board. ◀ There is a wooden railing along the path on the left and white houses on the right. Descend via stairs with hotel buildings and a fence on the right. Arrive at **Praia Vale de Centeanes** about 30min after the lighthouse. It is a great beach to stop for a swim.

From Praia Vale de Centeanes you can retrace your steps to Praia da Marinha (probably it will take you less than 2hr). Or you can continue to Ferragudo (Walk 21).

WALK 21

Praia Vale de Centeanes to Ferragudo

Start	Praia Vale de Centeanes (N37.091648, W8.453881)
Finish	Ferragudo, Castelo de São João de Arade
Distance	12km
Total ascent	245m
Total descent	235m
Grade	3
Time	4hr–4hr 30min
Refreshments	Beach restaurant at Praia Vale de Centeanes and Praia dos Caneiros, restaurants and cafés at Praia Carvoeiro, snack bar at Praia da Pintadinho. Note that many of the beach cafés/restaurants are only open during the season, usually from May to October.
Access	Vale de Centeanes is located along the M530 road, which runs parallel to the coast. Turn towards the beach when you see the Vale de Centeanes beach sign. There is a parking area near the beach. If you are planning to take a bus from Ferragudo at the end of your walk, check the timetable locally before you set off.
Warning	Take care on the cliff-tops and don't get too close to the edge. Note that due to constant erosion, the trail may change from one year to the next.

On this stretch of the coastal path you can admire sinkholes, small rock-lined beaches and see a lighthouse before arriving at Ferragudo, where the Arade River meets the ocean.

The trail described finishes by the Castelo de São João de Arade. You can only admire the exterior of the building. From the castle you can choose to retrace your steps to Praia Vale de Centeanes (but allow enough time for the return) or to Carvoeiro.

The trail described is linear; however, it is possible to retrace your steps, but if planning to do so you should set off early to allow enough time for the walk.

The path starts by the '0 stop' bar sign, at the end of the car park, where steps lead to the beach. Instead of going down to the beach, climb up on the stony hillside by the '0 stop' bar sign. Soon arrive at a railing, and then continue with great views of the ocean and the beach down below on the left. There is a hotel building on the right. Junipers, rock roses and shrubs line the path. Look out for a sinkhole near the path and a sea stack near a small beach. This beach might only be accessible via the steep steps at low tide.

There is a deep, fenced sinkhole and then you descend towards a big hotel building. Walk by a fence, and notice the stairs leading down to the small beach (**Praia de Vale Covo**). Curve around the beach slightly uphill and then continue with great views to the ocean on your left and villas visible on your right. Follow the well-trodden path and arrive at a car park at **Algar Seco** (from here you can go down to explore the rocks). Continue on the boardwalk after the car park. ◂

You can follow some stairs down to the rocks near the ocean. Descend on narrow stairs carved into rocks and walk through a small tunnel.

At the end of the boardwalk, keep left on the pavement and arrive at **Nossa Senhora da Encarnação** church. From the church continue downhill and a few minutes later arrive at **Praia de Carvoeiro** (there are plenty of

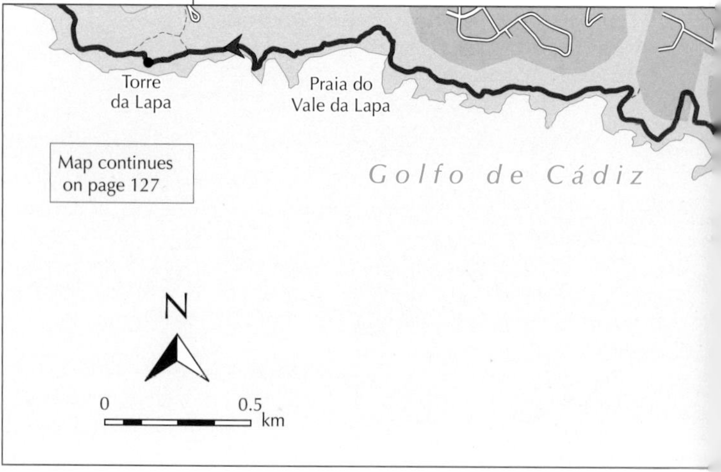

Coastal path towards Praia do Carvoeiro

cafés and restaurants here as well as a public toilet). If the weather allows this is a good place to stop for a swim and refreshments. With the beach behind you head towards the tourist information office and go left uphill by the building. Ascend on the tarmac with views to the beach on your left. Just before the road bends right, follow some steps to a small viewpoint by a ruined building. From here the path continues to the right (behind the ruins and fence). Continue on a rocky path with views to the left, and you can see the small rock-fringed **Praia do Paraíso**.

A deep ravine after Praia do Paraíso

Emerge back on the road by a restaurant. Keep left on the road; after the restaurant and car park, leave the road on a narrow path to the left. Walk beside a long fence and some railings. Descend to a ravine and continue on its other side. The path then runs close to the edge with great views. You will be walking beside a fence, and notice some villas on the right. When the fence turns inland, stay on the path along the cliff. Descend steeply to the ravine, then climb up on its other side.

There is a network of paths, but continue along the cliffs for great views. Descend into another ravine then climb up the other side. Walk along the cliffs with the ocean on the left and some villas on the right further inland. Walk on a stony plateau and notice the ruin of a small house near the path, keep close to the edge for great views. Not far in the distance, you can see a small stone tower on a cliff. Take any of the paths, but try to stay parallel to the line of the cliffs to enjoy some great views. ◄ You can admire some cliffs and coves if you

Small boats often sail up and down the coast to admire the coastline from the sea.

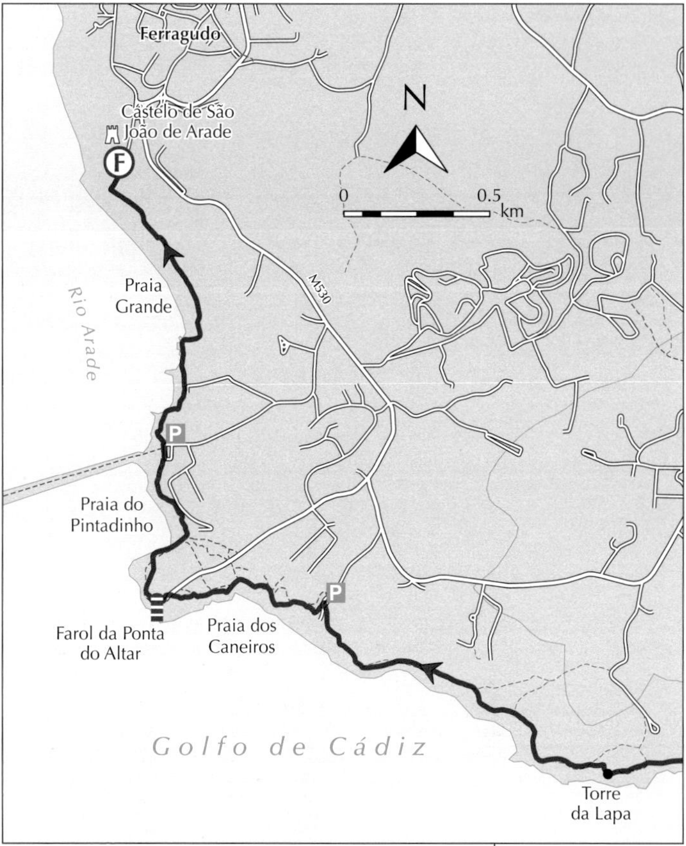

take the path closer to the edge, but take extra care. Head towards the small tower (**Torre da Lapa**).

From the tower, continue along the cliffs. Portimão comes into view and Lagos is also visible further down the coastline. **Farol da Ponta do Altar** (lighthouse) is visible on an outcrop. You might notice a ruined house on the right. Soon descend to **Praia dos Caneiros** (beach) car park. There is a restaurant here. Continue uphill by the

Colourful houses of Portimão marina on the opposite side of the Arade river

information board and soon you have great views to two sea stacks. Pass some huge sinkholes with railings and then arrive at the Farol da Ponta do Altar (lighthouse) car park in about 30–40min after Torre da Lapa.

Go around the fenced lighthouse, follow the path and shortly arrive at **Praia da Pintadinho**, a small beach with a snack bar. Continue uphill on the other side of the beach. The mouth of the **river Arade** is on the left. Walk along the river, and you can see the colourful houses of the marina on the other side of the river. Pass a villa on the right.

Emerge into a car park and continue on the pavement. There is a viewpoint here and the path continues by the restaurant. You can see Fóia and Picota in the background as you walk along the cliff towards a fort. Descend among bushes and go along a fence. Arrive at a long sandy beach. Walk the entire length of the beach and join a board walk at the far end. Climb the stairs on the right by a restaurant. Emerge into a car park and follow the road along the **Castelo de São João de Arade** walls. You can retrace your steps making it into a full-day walk or take a bus from Ferragudo to Portimão.

Castelo de São João de Arade (fort) was built in the 16th century to defend Portimão against attacks. It is closed to the public, you can only admire the mighty exterior.

WALK 22

Praia do Barranco das Canas short coast walk

Start/finish	Praia do Barranco das Canas car park, Portimão (N37.120628, W8.563721)
Distance	4.5km
Total ascent/descent	100m
Grade	1
Time	1hr 15min
Refreshments	None along the trail
Access	From the direction of Alvor on the Avenida das Comunidades Lusíadas (M531) take the Urbanização Vau da Rocha on the right. Follow to a car park area. Praia do Barranco das Canas is close to Praia do Vau.
Warning	Take care on the cliff-tops and don't get too close to the edge. Note that due to constant erosion, the trail may change from one year to the next.

This short coast walk gives endless opportunities to admire the coastline. It can be enjoyed as an easy afternoon stroll with plenty of photo opportunities. During the walk you can admire the craggy coast with sea stacks and sinkholes.

The sea is dotted with several **sea stacks** along this section of the coast. The scenery offers great photo opportunities and many people choose to admire the stacks from the cliffs, while others explore the coastline by boat. The waves slowly make their way into the cracks on the limestone rocks, gradually creating a cave. When the waves form a cave in a headland it can break through and form an arch, which then gradually grows until the top can no longer be supported. This then collapses, leaving a stack behind.

From **Praia do Barranco das Canas car park** take the wide track downhill. Near the beach, climb a narrow path by an information board and head west. You immediately

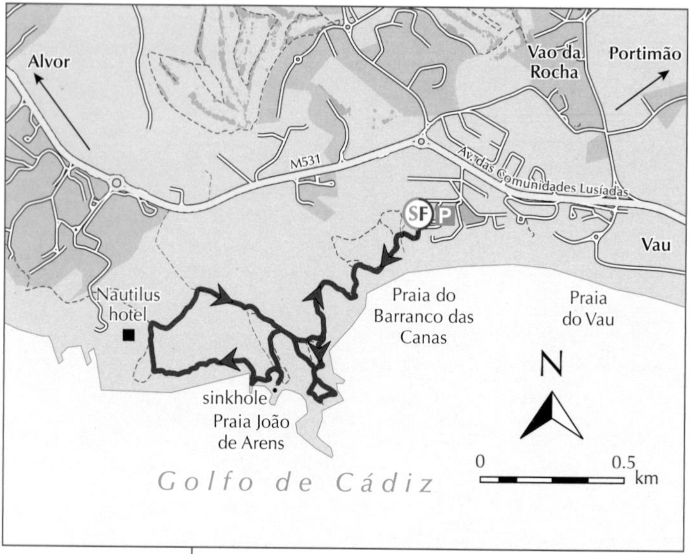

Arrive at a huge sinkhole

have views to the beach. Keep left and with the ocean on your left follow the path on the cliffs. You have endless opportunities to admire the craggy coastline and the numerous sea stacks near the cliffs. There is a network of well-trodden footpaths, try to keep closer to the edge for great views. There are many outcrops you can walk out to, to marvel at the coastline.

Reach a building and a huge **sinkhole** with railing. Peek down from a small metal bridge. And then continue along the fence. Notice a small beach, Praia do Submarino on the left. At the end of the fence, keep right inland. When the path splits, go right amongst eucalyptus and pine trees. Emerge onto a field, and go right. Notice some houses on the left with the silhouette of Fóia in the background. Arrive on a road and bear right. There are villas on the right and a field to the left. Take the path parallel to the road towards the ocean just after the house on the left. When it splits, take the left branch, and soon arrive back on the coastal path, where you keep left to retrace your steps to the car park.

Sinkholes are often not fenced off so take good care!

WALK 23

Alvor boardwalk

Start/finish	Alvor marina, fishermen's huts (N37.126453, W8.596026)
Distance	5km
Total ascent/descent	10m
Grade	1
Time	1hr 15min
Refreshments	Cafés, bars, restaurants in Alvor. Restaurant on Alvor beach.
Access	Marginal de Alvor (road) on the seafront. There are plenty of places to park.

This is a very easy stroll on boardwalks and on a sandy beach. The boardwalk is built to protect an important environment – the dunes. The Alvor Wetland is home to many birds and migrating birds also stop here. During this pleasant circular walk, you can observe different species inhabiting the area where the marshland meets the ocean. You don't have to follow the signs strictly, but if you do you will complete an almost 5km circular walk.

An information board marks the beginning of the trail at the car park. Follow the wooden boardwalk and keep right as the (PR) yellow/red sign indicates. There are **observation platforms** and information boards located along the boardwalk.

You can enjoy the views towards the fishing port and the wetland. Four small rivers feed the wetlands and join the ocean.

◂ Follow the boardwalk and ignore a branch on the left to carry straight on. Keep left on the next boardwalk and when you reach a sandy path go right. Continue along the sandy path that eventually takes you to the **Praia do Alvor** (beach). Reach the beach approximately 40min after starting from the car park. Keep left and walk along the sandy beach. You can enjoy some great views of the ocean and towards the buildings of Alvor. From the beach, rejoin the boardwalk again on the left. Follow

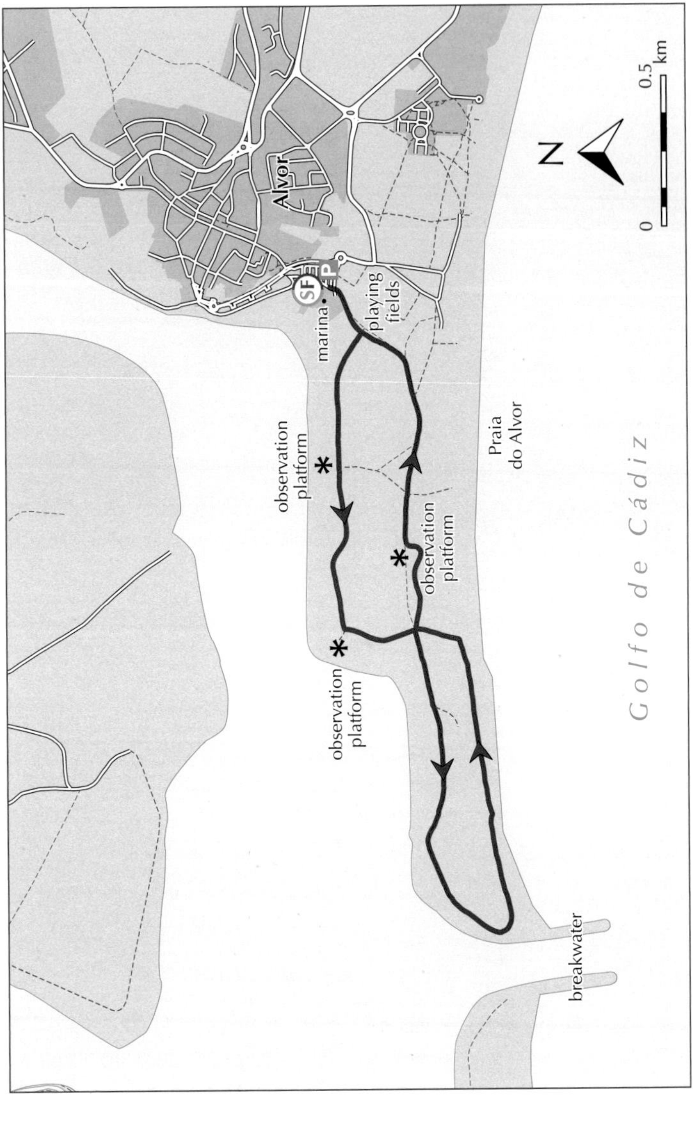
N
0
0.5
km
Alvor
SF
P
marina
playing fields
observation platform
observation platform
observation platform
Praia do Alvor
Golfo de Cádiz
breakwater

The houses of Alvor in the distance

the board walk and keep right when the yellow/red sign indicates. Soon you arrive back at the sandy path, where keep right. At the intersection carry straight on, shortly you reach the boardwalk again, and follow it back to the car park.

Please note that you can explore the boardwalks and the beach in different ways, but it is important to stick to the boardwalk and the signposted paths as it is intended to protect the fragile environment.

Dom João II, king of Portugal, ruled the country for 14 years from 1481. He died in 1495 in **Alvor**. The small fishing town was almost completely destroyed in the 1755 earthquake, but you can still see the remains of the Igreja Matriz, a 16th century church. Tourists started to discover the sleepy fishing town in the 1960s. Today the town is a popular tourist destination, but the mainly low-rise buildings have helped to retain its character.

WALK 24

Lagos to Luz

Start	Lagos: Praia Dona Ana car park, near Carvi Beach Hotel (N37.091320, W8.669762)
Finish	Luz, beach
Distance	10km
Total ascent	270m
Total descent	280m
Grade	2
Time	3hr–3hr 30min
Refreshments	Cafés and snack bars: at Praia Dona Ana car park, restaurant at the start of the path and at the car park of the Farol da Ponta da Piadede (lighthouse), and at Praia de Porto de Mós. Plus, there are plenty of cafés, restaurants and snack bars in Luz.
Access	In Lagos heading south on Estr. da Ponta da Piedade, turn left onto Alameda Dr. Armando Soares Ribeiro towards Praia Dona Ana. There are plenty of places to park near the beach. If you are planning to take a bus from Luz at the end of your walk, check the timetable locally before you set off. There are buses from Praia de Porto de Mós and from Luz.
Warning	Take care on the cliff-tops and don't get too close to the edge. Note that due to constant erosion, the trail may change from one year to the next.

This walk follows the coastline with extensive views. Near Lagos the stunning yellow sea stacks are washed with turquoise water, further along the trail, the ground is often reddish, and some stubborn, green vegetation grows on the wind-exposed cliffs. The colours are more intense on a sunny day, with the deep blue sky as background. There is an opportunity to stop for a swim along the trail or in Luz.

The trail described is linear; however, it is possible to retrace your steps. On the return, you most probably won't follow the cliffs so strictly and can cut off some outcrops; therefore you can get back to Lagos significantly faster (approximately 2hr).

This route can also be extended into a long, more demanding full-day walk by continuing with Walk 25 to Salema. The coastal path between Lagos and Cabo de São Vicente (Walk 24–27) can be walked as a three or four-day trek, with accommodation available in towns and villages along the trail.

From Praia Dona Ana car park follow the tarmac road uphill by hotel buildings. The left side of the road is private property and is fenced off. Arrive at Estrada da Ponta da Piedade, go left and follow the road for a few minutes. There are further snack bars and restaurants along this road.

Keep left towards Restaurante o Camilo. There is a car park by this **restaurant** near the cliffs. Steps lead down to a small beach just behind the building, but keep right, opposite the restaurant on a dirt path. Alternatively, you can walk to the end of the car park and look out for a path starting near the cliffs and keep right on that path. ◄ Follow this narrow path along the cliffs with the ocean on your left. Take extra care as the rocks are constantly eroding; after rain you can often see new, loose parts.

From the end of the car park you have some great views of the jagged coastline with many sea stacks towards Lagos.

As on the other sections of the coast, there is a network of footpaths running mainly parallel to the ocean. You can choose almost any of the paths as long as you stay safely away from the edge. Some paths run down to gullies and then climb back up, some snake to small outcrops offering better views, while others try to avoid any downhill and uphill sections. Soon after the start, a lighthouse and a radar post come into view in front of you.

Head towards the lighthouse on one of the paths with the ocean on your left. Arrive at the **Farol da Ponta da Piadede** (lighthouse) about 20–30min (dependent on which path you take) after leaving Restaurante o Camilo car park. There is a car park and a small restaurant here. Go around the lighthouse and continue on a paved path. You can follow this, or one of the footpaths closer to the coastline for better views.

About 15min after the lighthouse, walk across a wooden bridge. Shortly, there is a viewpoint with a platform and a bench along the path. (The small paths occasionally meet the surfaced path.) On reaching an unfinished – at the time of writing – building, you have a choice between going downhill on the eroded steps and continuing on the crumbling path along the fence, or skipping the eroded section and instead walking on surfaced roads.

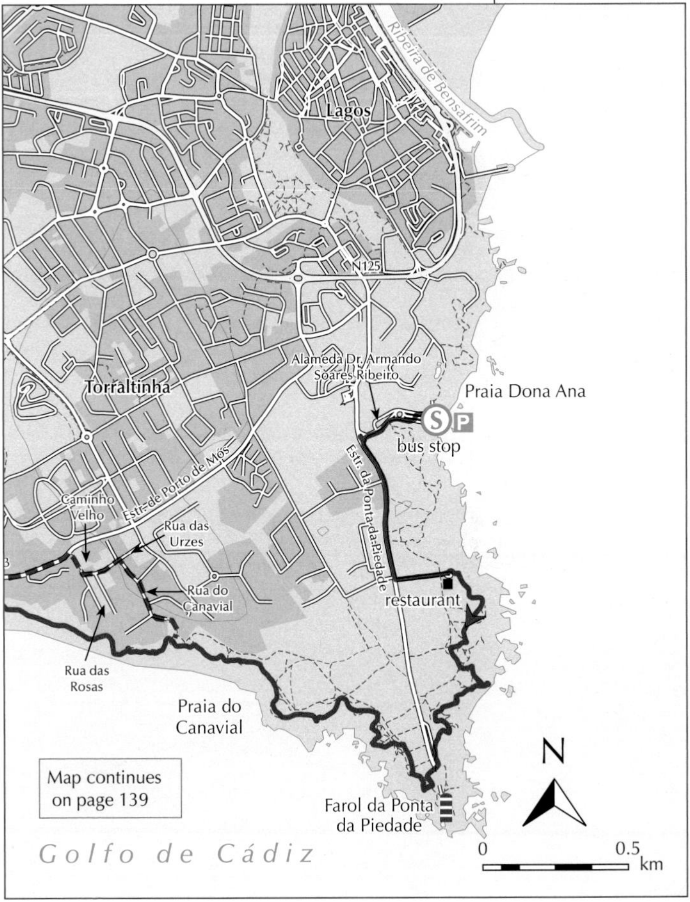

Coastal route (eroded)

Keep left after the unfinished building and descend on the worn-out steps to a small, hidden stony beach and then continue uphill on the narrow eroded path. There are villas on your right and the ocean on your left. Walk along the fence and then descend to a long stony beach; **Praia de Porto de Mós** (about 1hr from the lighthouse). There is a car park, restaurant, toilet, and bus stop here.

Alternative section on streets

You can continue on the surfaced path by the unfinished building by keeping slightly right just before reaching the stairs, and shortly arriving at a small car park. From there, follow the Rua do Cannavia and reach Rua das Urzes in a T-junction. Turn left and in the next T-junction turn right onto Caminho Velho, reach a major road (M1263) keep left and walk down to **Praia de Porto de Mós**.

Fóia and Picota are also visible in the distance.

The coastal path continues after Praia de Porto de Mós car park. Go uphill by a restaurant (Antonio's). The beach is down below on your left and there are some villas on your right. ◂ Carry straight on along the cliffs. Soon reach a railing on the left and notice a plantation on the right. Ahead there are views towards Luz. About 50min after leaving Praia de Porto de Mós, arrive at a large concrete **trig point**. The path goes downhill from here. Follow the

narrow path towards a modern villa and then keep left towards Luz (there are several paths and some of them are steeper than others). Head towards the buildings and arrive at a cobbled road. Descend between villas and arrive at **Luz beach** and its promenade.

Farol da Ponta da Piadede (lighthouse) comes into sight

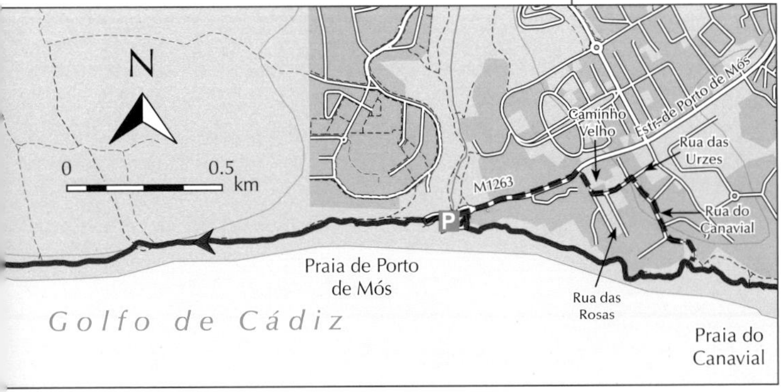

Praia da Luz is in the distance

From Luz you can retrace your steps to Lagos, take a bus back, or you can book a night in Luz. Alternatively, this section of the coastal path can be extended to a longer day walk by continuing to Salema (Walk 25). It is recommended that you book accommodation before you arrive, especially during the late spring and summer months.

WALK 25

Luz to Salema

Start	Luz, car park at the beach front (N37.087481, W8.726750)
Finish	Salema, car park at the beach front
Distance	13km
Total ascent	250m
Total descent	260m
Grade	3
Time	4hr–4hr 30min
Refreshments	Restaurants, cafés at Luz, Burgau, Praia das Cabanas Velhas and Salema.
Access	From the direction of Lagos take the N125 road westwards then take the M537. Reaching Luz, take Rua Alfredo do Nascimento Batista, and at the end of the road turn right into Rua Luz Bayclub and follow the 'praia' signs down to the beachfront with a car park. If you are planning to take a bus from Salema at the end of your walk, check the timetable locally before you set off.
Warning	Take care on the cliff-tops and don't get too close to the edge. Note that due to constant erosion, the trail may change from one year to the next.

Follow the coastal path and enjoy great views, visit a small fortress and imagine the time when it had an important role in protecting the fishing industry from pirates. You will cross a rushing river. The low hill after the crossing is a great place to spot orchids in the springtime. Salema was a small fishing village, but today its remarkable beach attracts plenty of tourists every year.

The trail described is linear; however it is possible to retrace your steps if you set off early. On the return, you most probably can get back to Luz significantly faster. If you are planning to stay in Salema, book your accommodation ahead.

Walk along the promenade in Luz. When you reach the **Fortaleza da Luz** (fort), keep right, pass the church and turn left on the first road (Rua da Calheta).

The well-trodden coastal path near Luz

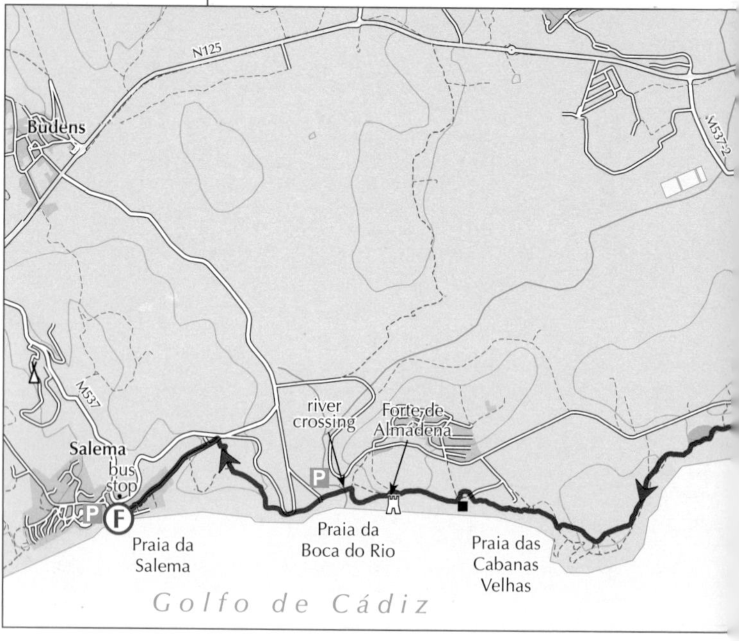

This road becomes a wide dirt track, and continues with some villas on the right and the ocean on the left. About 20min from the start, the dirt track narrows down to a path. Carry straight on, with further villas on your right, following the contour of the coast. There are – as always – a couple of other paths running along the coast. Take care and don't venture too close to the cliff edge. There are villas overlooking the ocean as you walk towards a small hill. Climb up the hill and from the top you can enjoy views of the coastline. Descend on the other side of the hill and continue along the coast. The coastline stretches out in front of you. Notice the remains of a windmill, on a small hill on the right.

About 1hr 20min from the fort of Luz, arrive at **Burgau** village by a restaurant building (Restaurant O Navegador). From the restaurant follow the road

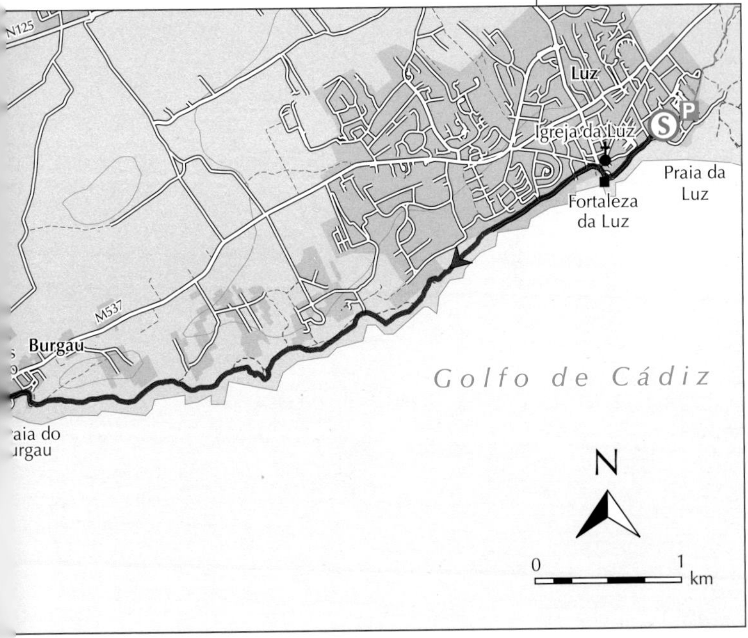

downhill. The road is lined with restaurants, cafés, and small hotels. Arrive at a small square near the beach, with further restaurants and cafés. Follow the road and go right uphill, arrive at a junction with a bus stop (Rua Principal). Keep left, (with a bus stop on your right,) and pass a fenced sports field.

Follow this road for about 5min and look out for a path starting on the left about 70m after Rua da Falésia (street on the left) at the zebra crossing. Leave the road on this path, go around a garden and continue west along the coastal path. On your right you can see a row of apartments with pools and the snaking road. Follow the undulating path along the cliffs with some great views. You can see Praia das Cabanas Velhas and Salema in the distance. You might notice some ruins near the water on the hillside.

About 50–60min after leaving Burgau, after a steep downhill section, arrive at **Praia das Cabanas Velhas** by

Undulating path near Burgau

a restaurant. Continue steeply uphill on the other side of the small beach. Pine trees populate the area alongside the path. ▸ Soon a fort appears on the horizon. Reach a fence and then descend along it, and arrive on a driveway. Cross the driveway and continue on its other side. Go around the house and then continue along the cliffs. Arrive at the **Forte de Almádena** (fort of Almádena) about 25min after leaving Praia das Cabanas Velhas. There is a small parking area and an information board here.

You can see a group of houses on the nearby hillside on the right with Fóia and Picota in the distant background.

Almádena Fort was built by the Count of Prado, governor and captain general of Algarve in 1632, to defend local fishing from pirate attacks. It is believed that the fort was built on a Roman temple dedicated to Neptune.

The fort housed four to six soldiers, and the small chapel was used as a watchtower. Very little is known about the fort's history as it was in ruins by the 19th century.

You can wander among the ruins of the fort. From the ruins continue downhill and reach a river as it meets the ocean. There is no bridge, you have to find the best crossing point, which is a lot easier at low tide. Most probably you will have to take your shoes off to cross, if you can't find suitable rocks to hop on. Ford the river and pass a small car park and information board and continue uphill along the cliffs. There are junipers here, and in the spring look out for orchids. Soon Salema's houses appear. Follow the path (it splits, but you can follow either branch) and emerge onto a tarmac road about 20–30min after crossing the river. Turn left and follow it for about 750m. Soon it turns into a cobbled road leading down to the **Praia da Salema** (beach).

There are restaurants, shops, and a car park near the beach. There is also a bus stop from where you can get a bus towards Sagres or Lagos. Alternatively you can retrace your steps making the trail into a long, but rewarding, full-day walk. ▸

You can walk back to Luz in about 2hr 40min.

WALK 26

Salema to Sagres

Start	Salema, car park at the beach front (N37.065499, W8.824897)
Finish	Sagres, tourist information office.
Distance	17km
Total ascent	400m
Total descent	395m
Grade	3
Time	5hr 30min–6hr
Refreshments	Restaurants and cafés in Salema and Sagres. Beach restaurants at Praia do Zavial and Praia da Ingrina.
Access	From the N125 road take the M537, which will take you down to Praia da Salema. There is a bus service between Lagos and Salema. Check the timetable locally before you set off. Some buses stop along the road, outside Salema (it is called 'Salema X' in the timetable). This stop is about 20min's walk from Salema's centre.
Warning	Take care on the cliff-tops and don't get too close to the edge. Note that due to constant erosion, the trail may change from one year to the next.

This trail is the longest section of the coastal path and is not waymarked. (There is a plan to extend the waymarked western coastal path, but this had not been done at the time of writing). Some sections of the trail are not suitable if you suffer from vertigo, and it is not recommended to walk it in strong winds or in bad weather. There is a network of paths running along the coast; always try to keep parallel to the coastline. The sound of crashing waves and fine views accompany you throughout the walk. There are several beaches along the trail.

The trail described is linear; and this section is probably too long to retrace your steps, therefore you will most probably have to take a bus from Sagres or stay for the night. It is recommended to set off early and make plans for how you will get back: if you are planning to take a bus from Sagres, check the timetable locally before you set off.

From the car park, walk away from the beach, along the rainwater channel and then keep left. Then take the first available street on the left again. Pass a football pitch. About 10min after leaving the car park, arrive at a viewpoint with benches and another car park. Look out for a narrow path starting on the left hand side of the pavement. Follow this, with villas on the right and the ocean on the left. The narrow, rocky path runs over the cliffs with fantastic views to the coastline.

Very soon you leave the villas behind and views open up to the shrub-covered coastal hills. About 15min after joining the narrow path, descend towards a small beach. Walk across it, and continue uphill on the other side. There are other trails as well; you can keep closer to the cliff edge for better views but take care. Or alternatively choose a different path running parallel, at a safer distance. ▶

The views are dominated by the coast, green, shrub-covered hills and the turquoise ocean.

The ocean is slowly claiming back the coast and there is evidence of this along the coastline. About 15–20min after the small beach, arrive at the **Forte de Vera Cruz da Figueira**.

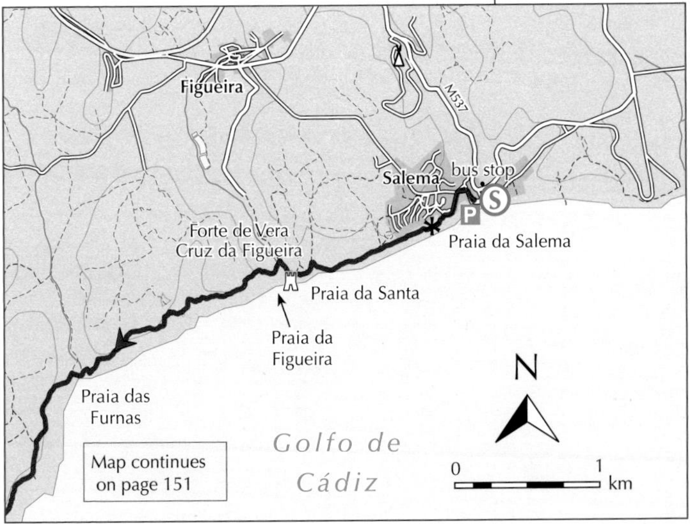

Map continues on page 151

Forte de Vera Cruz da Figueira was part of a line of forts along the cliffs, and from here, signals were sent to Almádena fort. In 1755 it was damaged by the earthquake, and the erosion of the cliffs have also weakened it. Today a small ruin is all that is left.

You can enjoy some great views towards the long, sandy **Praia da Figueira** (beach). From the ruins, descend to a riverbed, cross some rocks and carry straight on. You might see some painted red spots on some rocks as the path continues steeply uphill. After the climb, it levels off for a while. Follow the path along the cliffs, with shrubs on your right while the coastline stretches out in front of you. Soon another sandy beach appears below. Descend to a ravine with a beach on the left. From this ravine continue uphill, then soon descend to another ravine. (Usually there is a path in every ravine leading to a beach, but the trail always continues uphill on the other side of the ravine, parallel to the ocean.)

The path can be overgrown in places. As you climb uphill again, the path runs among shrubs and you might notice the remains of a drystone wall. ◂ You can see some wind turbines in the distance.

Juniper, rock roses, and wild rosemary populate the hills.

Descend steeply to **Praia das Furnas** (beach) about 50–60min after leaving the ruins of the fort. Then continue uphill at the other end of the beach. At first scramble uphill over rocks and then the path levels out.

Pass the remains of a drystone wall. Looking back, you can see all the way back to Luz.

There is a network of paths; keep the ocean on your left and choose the most suitable one. Occasionally you might come across a red spot, marking (unofficially) the coastal path. For the best coastal views, choose the path closer to the cliff edge, but at a safe distance from the drop. Reach a wider path, and when this splits, carry straight on. Keep on the well-trodden wide track and soon you have the first views of **Praia do Zavial** (beach). Descend to the beach about 30min after leaving Praia das Furnas. There is a restaurant and a car park here. You can walk across the beach or follow the narrow path parallel to it.

Views towards Praia da Figueira

At the western end of the beach, a rocky path starts uphill. Walk along the edge, with great views. Pass a house on the hill on the right. Enjoy more views towards the coast and then descend towards the next small beach. Cross a dirt track and continue on its other side. Arrive at **Praia da Ingrina** car park with a restaurant about 20min after leaving Praia do Zavial. Go around the restaurant building and continue on the wooden bridge with the beach on your left. At the end of the bridge, keep left on the road by an **old warehouse**.

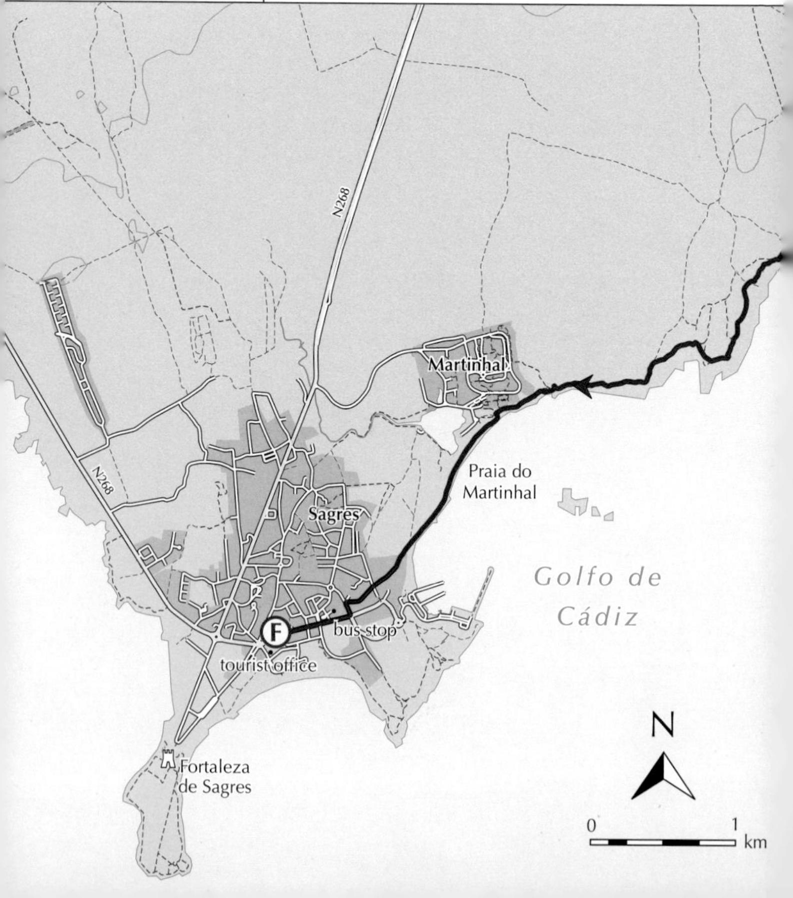

There is a parking area for caravans and a small path starts from a dirt track after that. Head towards the coastline (you can join this path later on but if you stay on the wide track you will get further from the coastline). Try to find a path close to the shoreline (there is a network of paths) and enjoy views of the dramatic coastline as you continue. Follow the contour of the coast with great views and you might notice a ramshackle building.

Praia do Barranco soon appears. Descend to this beach and walk across it. Find a narrow sandy path leading to the rocks, and then climb the rocky path uphill. Try to keep safely away from the cliff edge but still relatively close for the best views. Follow the contour of the coast on the shrub-covered flat area with views of the dramatic coast. The buildings of Sagres appear in the distance about 50min–1hr after leaving

Steep ascent at Praia das Furnas

Praia do Barranco. There is a ruined building on the hill on the right. There are many paths and the route is not signposted; try to keep parallel to the ocean as much as possible as you head towards Sagres. You can see an old farmhouse on the right, and look out for sinkholes. Try to find the most well-trodden path.

Dramatic views and sinkholes dominate this section.

◀ Head towards the buildings of Sagres. Descend to a beach with a small river, walk across the small sandy beach, and climb uphill on its other side. There are some villas on the right, and soon arrive at a long sandy beach. There is a beach snack bar/restaurant here. Walk the entire length of the beach and then continue on a dirt track towards the buildings. Continue away from the beach with the port on the left.

Arrive at the town, carry straight on then keep left, and then take the first right to reach the tourist information office. You can take a bus back to Salema or Luz, but check the timetable as not all the buses stop at Salema. Some stop along the N125 road, near Salema from where you can walk down to Salema centre in about 20min.

WALK 27

Sagres to Cabo de São Vicente

Start	Sagres, tourist information office (N37.007849, W8.940450)
Finish	Cabo de São Vicente
Distance	10km
Total ascent	255m
Total descent	225m
Grade	2
Time	3hr
Refreshments	Cafés and snack bars in Sagres, roadside restaurants along the route and pop-up stands at Cabo de São Vicente.
Access	Sagres is located on the N268 road, which is accessible from the N125 road. There is a bus service between Lagos and Sagres, but check the timetable locally. There is a car park near the tourist information office. If you are planning to take a bus from Cabo de São Vicente at the end of your walk check the timetable locally before you set off.
Warning	Take care on the cliff-tops and don't get too close to the edge. Note that due to constant erosion, the trail may change from one year to the next.

Follow the dramatic coastline to Europe's south westernmost point. Battered by strong winds and shaped by the forceful waves, this was considered the end of the known world until the 14th century. Cabo de São Vicente (Cape St Vincent) with its lighthouse perched on rocks, attracts many people so it can get a bit busy. It is also the finishing point of the Via Algarviana (GR13) and Rota Vicentina long-distance trails.

The trail described is linear; however, it is possible to retrace your steps to get back to Sagres.

Start walking with the square and the tourist information office on your left. At the roundabout keep straight towards **Fortaleza de Sagres** (fort), and at the next roundabout carry straight on towards Cabo de São Vicente. Leaving Sagres

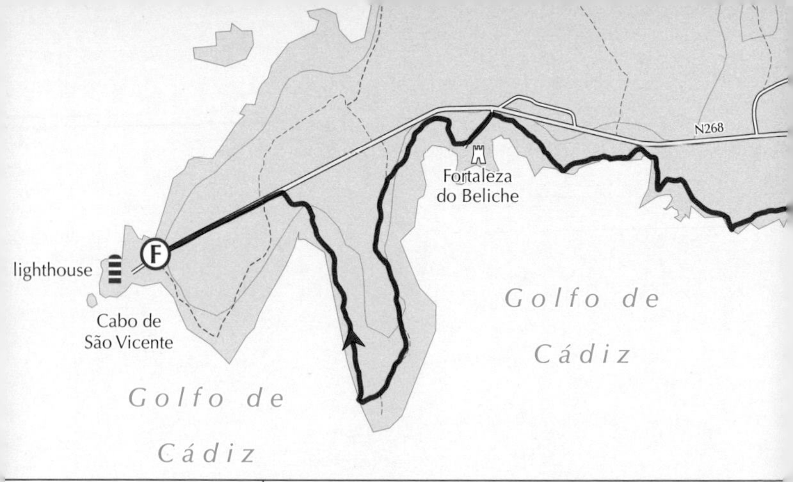

There are some sinkholes, so take care.

behind, walk by a fenced **military area**. Leave the road to the left after the fenced area (1.5km from Sagres centre). Head towards the ocean, and then with the ocean on your left follow the coastline along one of the footpaths. The road is visible on your right. ◂ The limestone coast stretches into the distance. The huge cracks and sinkholes are reminders of just how fragile the coast is. There are views towards a fort and Cape St Vincent as you follow the rocky, stony path along the coastline.

The rugged limestone coastline stretches into the distance

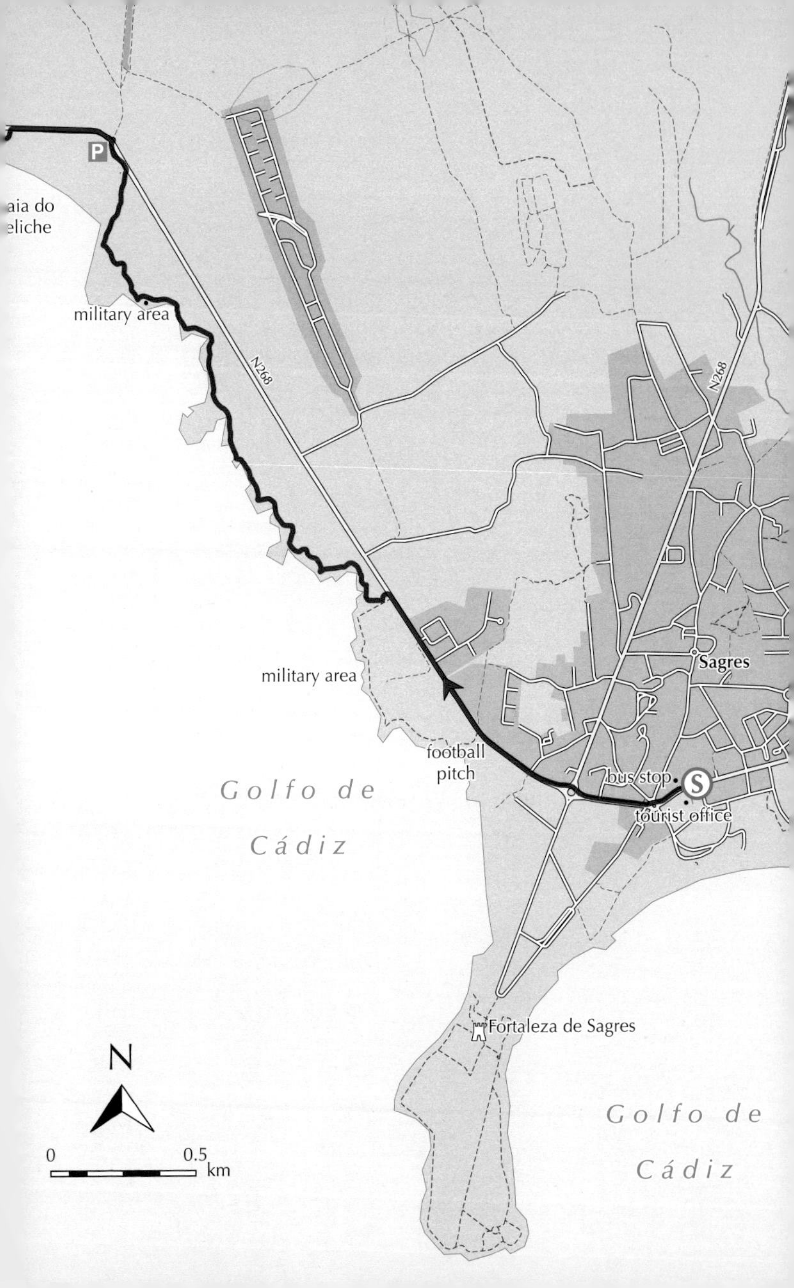
aia do
eliche
military area
N268
military area
Sagres
N268
football
pitch
bus stop
S
tourist office
Golfo de
Cádiz
Fortaleza de Sagres
N
0
0.5
km
Golfo de
Cádiz

You might see some cars parked near the cliffs, and if you observe the rocks carefully, you can see local **fishermen** standing on small rocky outcrops, trying to catch something for dinner. It is a mystery how they got to the outcrop in the first place.

There are some houses on the right alongside the road, but otherwise the views are dominated by the shrub-lined path, the coastline and the ocean. Reach a fenced **military area** about 30min after the first fenced area. You can go around the fence either way. As you continue along the coast, the lighthouse at Cape St Vincent comes into sight. Follow the well-trodden path and soon the rock-fringed Praia do Beliche (beach) appears below. It is popular with surfers.

Follow the coastline and reach a car park by the road. There is also a restaurant here. Continue on the tarmac road after the car park. Ignore a very faint, overgrown,

The lighthouse of Cabo de São Vicente comes into view

narrow path on the left. A few minutes later leave the tarmac road to the left on a wide path towards the ocean. Follow the well-trodden path and enjoy some great views towards a fort clinging on the rocks. The lighthouse is also distinguishable in the distance.

> As you follow the coastline, look out for great rock formations. You can also observe the **layered rocks**; it looks as if a giant has spread different layers of mud and rocks on top of each other.

▶ Occasionally the path swings closer to the road as you walk towards the fort. Arrive at a restaurant by the road near **Fortaleza do Beliche**, about 50–60min after Praia do Beliche.

Juniper populates the area near the path.

You can enjoy further views from the fort, but the trail continues towards the **lighthouse**. There is a path near the road, but the more scenic route runs along

Lighthouse of Cabo de São Vicente

the coastline. This takes you out to the small peninsula, from where you can enjoy some great views of the fort and the ocean. If you follow this route it will take you about 40min to reach the tarmac road again. When you do, keep left and follow it to the lighthouse. There is a bus stop, pop-up snack bars and a car park near the lighthouse.

After visiting the lighthouse and/or spending some time admiring the jagged coast you can retrace your steps or walk back on the N268 road (about 6km to Sagres), or take a bus back to Sagres. Note that there are only two buses daily from Cabo de São Vicente to Sagres, so make sure you have the necessary information about the local buses before you set off. Alternatively you can extend the walk by following Walk 28.

COSTA VICENTINA

You can admire the characteristic rocks of Praia do Telheiro on Walk 28

COSTA VICENTINA

Descending towards Praia do Cardoama on Walk 29

The west coast is less developed and is cooler than the rest of the Algarve; it is constantly battered by strong winds and many of the small beaches are popular with surfers. Once, Cabo de São Vicente (Walk 28) was believed to be the end of the known world. Today, many people visit the lighthouse and stare towards the vast Atlantic Ocean. Leaving Cabo de São Vicente behind, the west coast feels a lot more remote and somehow less busy than the south coast. But every year, more and more people follow the Rota Vicentina and the other trails in the west, and the area is increasingly popular; therefore many of the small villages cater for tourists.

Salema or **Sagres** can be a good base to explore the west coast. Salema still has the charm of a fishing village, with a beautiful beach and some seafood restaurants. Sagres might be less busy than other big coastal towns in the Algarve, but booking ahead is recommended. Those who would prefer a smaller and quieter place and have their own transport might choose **Vila do Bispo** as a base for exploring the west coast. There are some restaurants in the small town and many of the trails described are easily accessible.

WALK 28

Cabo de São Vicente–Praia do Telheiro circular

Start/finish	Cabo de São Vicente (N37.023409, W8.995504)
Distance	10km
Total ascent/descent	120m
Grade	2
Time	2hr 30min–3hr
Refreshments	Pop-up snack bars at Cabo de São Vicente.
Access	From Sagres follow the N268 road to Cabo de São Vicente. There are two daily buses to and from Sagres of which one continues to Lagos. Sagres centre is only about 6km from Cabo de São Vicente on the N268 road. Alternatively, you can combine this walk with Walk 27 for a full-day walk. First follow the walk as described in Walk 27, then continue to Praia do Telheiro, and on the return section on reaching the tarmac road, go left and follow it back to Sagres. From Sagres there are regular bus services along the coast to Lagos. If you are planning to use buses, check the timetable and seek information locally before you set off.

From the lighthouse of Cabo de São Vicente, follow the often sandy path along the coast and enjoy the great views to Telheiro Beach. This windswept part of the Algarve is well-visited, but once you leave the lighthouse behind, sandy paths, rugged landscapes, rocks and shrubs dominate the scenery.

The **Cabo de São Vicente** is named after the martyred 4th century deacon St Vicente whose body – according to legend – was brought ashore here. There was a Franciscan monastery here, that paid homage to St Vicente, but the original buildings were destroyed by the 1755 earthquake. The lighthouse – built on the ruins of the monastery – began operating in 1846.

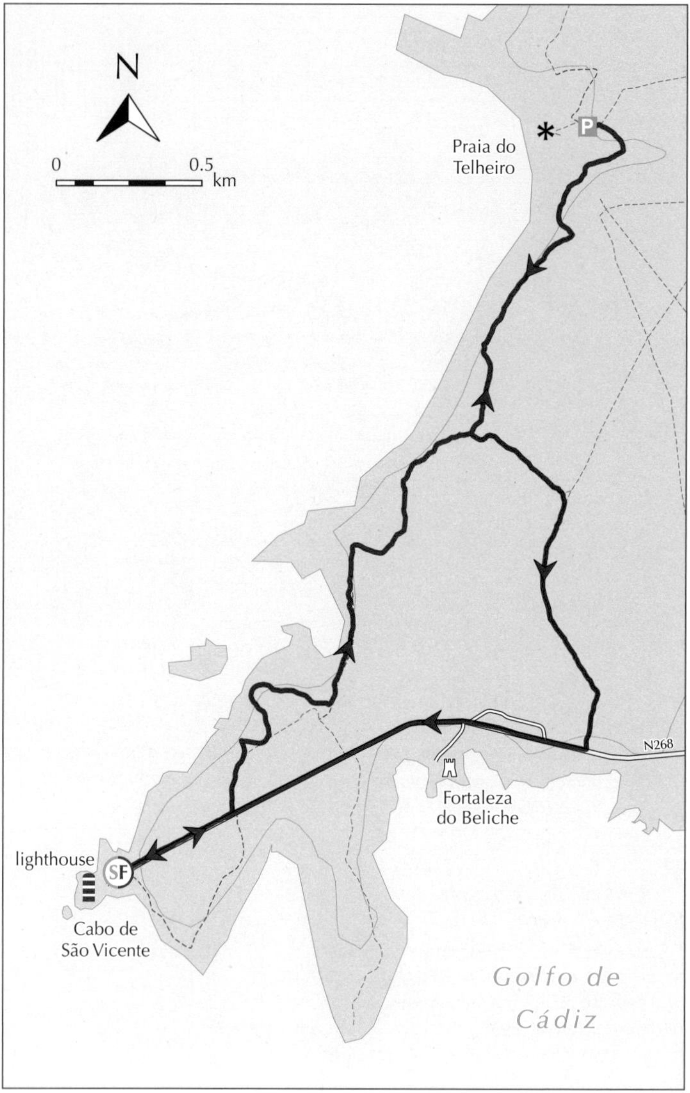
N
0
0.5
km
Praia do
Telheiro
N268
Fortaleza
do Beliche
lighthouse
SF
Cabo de
São Vicente
Golfo de
Cádiz

Walkers on the rocky path near Cabo de São Vicente

Start on the tarmac road (N268) with the **lighthouse** behind you. Leave the tarmac road to the left as the white/red sign indicates. A few minutes later, at the junction keep left on the path marked with a white/red cross, closer to the coast (the white/red marked trail continues straight on). Soon, you follow a wide path with views to the coast on your left. Before long, spot a green/blue sign (Fishermen's trail) and continue on the rocky path. ▶

There are signs and cairns to help you navigate along this well-trodden route.

The characteristic red rocks come into view, and the lighthouse is visible behind you. Shrubs populate the area, as you continue with the vast ocean on your left. The ground soon turns to reddish sand. About an hour after leaving the lighthouse, you will have great views to **Praia do Telheiro** (beach). You can admire the characteristic red rocks from above. Descend to a ravine then climb up on its other side, and arrive at a clearing, used as a **parking area**. Further views can be enjoyed from the nearby viewpoint (slightly to the left) The trail continues as part of the long-distance Fishermen's Trail, however your route turns back from here.

The red rocks of Praia do Telheiro in the distance

An example of **geological unconformity** in western Europe can be seen at Telheiro Beach. Unconformity occurs when there is a gap in the geological record. It means a period of geological time – in this case about 50-90 million years – is not represented in the rock formation because the missing layer eroded away before the deposition of the new layer.

Admire the views, and then retrace your steps through the ravine. When you reach a wide path, follow it and join the dirt track on the left. Follow that track away from the lighthouse and about 20min after turning back, you can see the buildings of Sagres in the distance. Reach a dirt track, and keep right. You can see a restaurant building by the road. About 15min later, arrive at the tarmac road, turn right and follow it for 1.8km, back to the lighthouse. You will pass **Fortaleza do Beliche** (fort) along the way. Alternatively, you can go left on the tarmac road. Sagres centre is 4.3km away.

WALK 29

Castelejo circular

Start/finish	Picnic area with car park along the M1265 road about 2km north-west of Vila do Bispo (N37.091329, W8.932224)
Distance	11km
Total ascent/descent	290m
Grade	2
Time	3hr–3hr 30min
Refreshments	Restaurant at Castelejo Beach and Praia da Cordoama
Access	Vila de Bispo is located where the N125 and N268 roads meet. From the village take the M1265 and about 2km from the village the picnic site is located on the left hand side of the road.

The first part of the walk (Trilho ambiental do Castelejo) is a short, signposted trail through a wooded area. This first section is easy to follow and can be enjoyed as a short afternoon stroll. In the early spring look out for orchids and enjoy some fine views. The trail described then takes you to Praia do Castelejo, and then along the cliffs with fine views before returning on a forest track. Two short sections of the walk follow tarmac roads.

Facing the barbecue area, keep left and follow the yellow/red signposted trail. Ignore a narrow trail immediately on the right. ▶ Mediterranean pines are the main vegetation alongside the track. Soon, notice a dirt track running parallel to the path, but keep right on the path and at the junction carry straight on.

The outline of Fóia is visible in the distance on your left.

Pass a disused **house**; go around the building and pass a small pond. Signs indicate the right way. Follow the wide path downhill, with a ravine on the right, while a concert of frogs might entertain you. There is a small pine-covered hill, on the left. About 15–20min after the house, arrive at a **small pond** with a picnic bench.

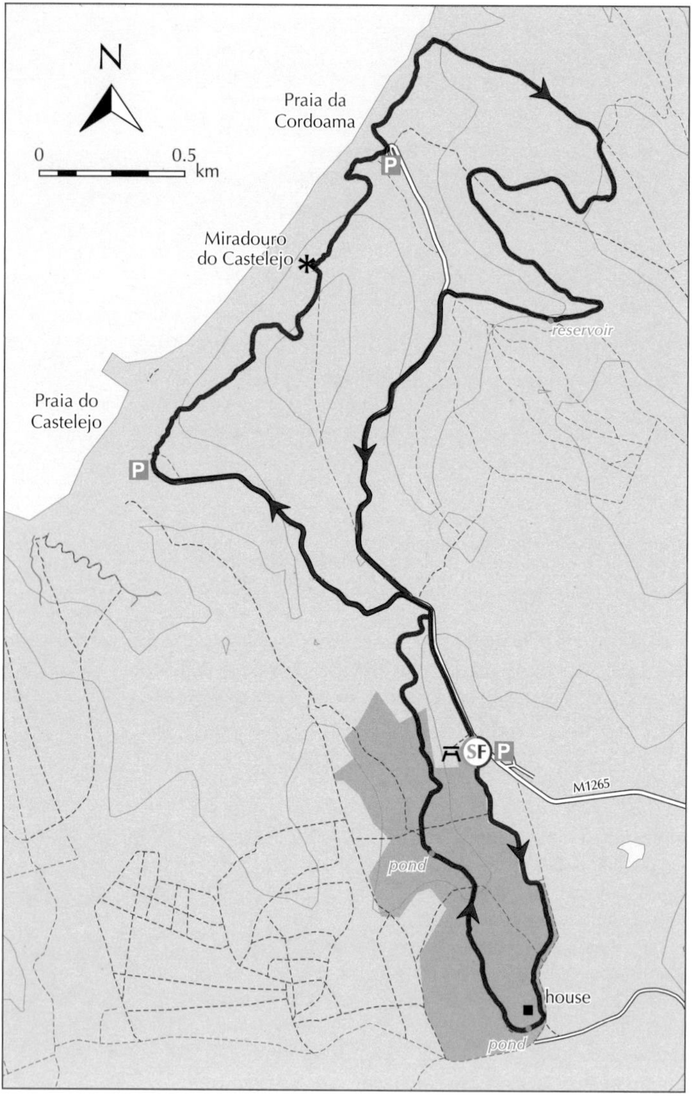
N
0
0.5
km
Praia da
Cordoama
P
Miradouro
do Castelejo
reservoir
Praia do
Castelejo
P
SF
P
M1265
pond
house
pond

Ignore a path on the left after the pond and continue straight on along the marked trail. There is a small ravine and a hill on the left. Soon views open up towards the ocean; you can spot a lone building on the hill on the left. Arrive at a tarmac road about an hour after leaving the picnic site.

Go left and about 100m later at the junction keep left downhill on the tarmac road towards the beach. Follow this narrow tarmac road for 1km downhill and arrive at **Praia do Castelejo**. There is a car park and a small restaurant here. Just before the restaurant building there are some steps leading steeply uphill on the right. Climb up these steps and follow the narrow path. Walk past a small building and continue uphill above the restaurant. As you follow the faint path, the beach is behind you, and you have views to the snaking road and hills on the right-hand side. Ascend steeply and soon the coastline stretches out in front of you. Heading slightly inland, go around a small ravine and then keep towards a viewpoint with railings. Arrive at the **Miradouro do Castelejo** (viewpoint) about 30min after leaving Praia Castelejo. From here you can enjoy great views in both directions.

From the viewpoint, join the yellow/red signposted trail going steeply downhill. Descend towards **Praia da Cordoama** (beach) and a restaurant. The path then bends towards the beach, crosses a river bed and arrives at a car park by the restaurant. Continue uphill by the restaurant as the yellow/red sign indicates. Climb for about 10min with the ocean on your left and enjoy some great views of the coastline. Then turn sharply right, inland. Walk along the small ridge, with ravines on both sides. The ocean is behind you, but its steady roar is a reminder of its presence.

At the junction, keep right on the forest track despite the fact that this is marked with a yellow/red cross (which usually means the path is not part of the marked trail). Follow this track slightly downhill through a pine forest. Ignore a track on the left and almost immediately, at the junction, keep right (the left track goes towards

The west coast is constantly battered by strong winds

Eucalyptus and pine trees populate the small slopes.

Vila do Bispo). There are some views towards the ocean on your right and you can also see the ridge you followed to the forest. Ignore a steep fire break on the right and continue on the track, bending slightly inland. You can spot the snaking tarmac and the viewpoint. ◂ Cross a stream, ignore a track on the left and carry straight on by a small **reservoir**. About 30min after joining the forest track marked with a yellow/red cross, arrive at a tarmac road. You can see the beach (Praia da Cordoama) with the restaurant on the right hand side. Keep left uphill and follow this tarmac road for about 20min. A dirt track forks off to the right towards the viewpoint, but stay on the tarmac road for a further 5min and arrive at a junction. Go left. You will recognise the path where you emerged onto this same road. There is a path running parallel to the road. Follow that for about 500m and arrive back at the **picnic site**.

WALK 30

Carrapateira circular

Start/finish	Carrapateira centre, from the bus stop (N37.183639, W8.895554)
Distance	12km
Total ascent/descent	165m
Grade	2
Time	3hr–3hr 30min but it depends on how many viewpoints you visit along the track.
Refreshments	Café/bar/restaurant, small supermarket in Carrapateira. There is a restaurant on the coast near Praia do Amado.
Access	Carrapateira is located along the N268 road about 13km north of Vila do Bispo. There is a small shop, bar/café and information board in the centre. A taxi is available, but try to make arrangements in advance.

Follow the signposted, well-trodden trail along the rugged, wind-battered coast. Take your time to enjoy the views of the rocky coastline from the wooden viewpoints while the sound of crashing waves and whistling wind accompany you. On the second part of this circular trail, there is a small archaeological site on the cliffs. You will then return to Carrapateira along tracks.

From the bus stop, go north towards the small hill with a windmill on top. Take the first left, with the windmill on the hill to your right. A green/blue sign marks the trail. (Pontal da Carrapateira).

Follow this minor asphalt road towards the dunes, leaving the buildings behind. Leave the road on the sandy path to the right, as the green/blue sign indicates. Soon the ocean comes into sight, while there are some villas on the right.

There is a **restaurant** on the right as you arrive at a tarmac road. Cross over and continue on the boardwalk starting on the other side of this road (signposted). Reach the Ribeira da Carrapateira (river) about 20min after leaving the village, and keep left on the signposted path. The river is on your right, and there are dunes nearby. Keep right by the area used by caravans. There are other paths, but follow the signs closer to the river. The sandy path is lined with shrubs and you have a view towards the ocean; Praia da Bordeira (beach) is on your right, with Carrapateira's houses behind you in the distance.

Reach some wooden steps, go left uphill and arrive at another boardwalk. You can make a short detour to the right to the first of many viewpoints to take in views of Bordeira beach. However, the trail continues straight on. Arrive at a small parking area, and keep right on the wide track towards the ocean. Continue and soon you have a chance to visit another viewpoint. The wide track follows the coastline, with the ocean on your right and rolling hills on the left. ◂ There are many viewpoints, usually wooden platforms on small outcrops from where you can admire the craggy landscape – characterised by the reddish rocks – battered by the strong wind. Looking back from one of the viewpoints, you can spot some wooden buildings perched on rocks. The signs indicate the right way; ignore a track on the left and keep closer to the ocean on the wide well-trodden track. Rolling hills dominate the horizon in front of you.

Shrubs grow stubbornly in this wind-exposed environment.

The Ribeira da Carrapateira joins the ocean at Bordeira beach

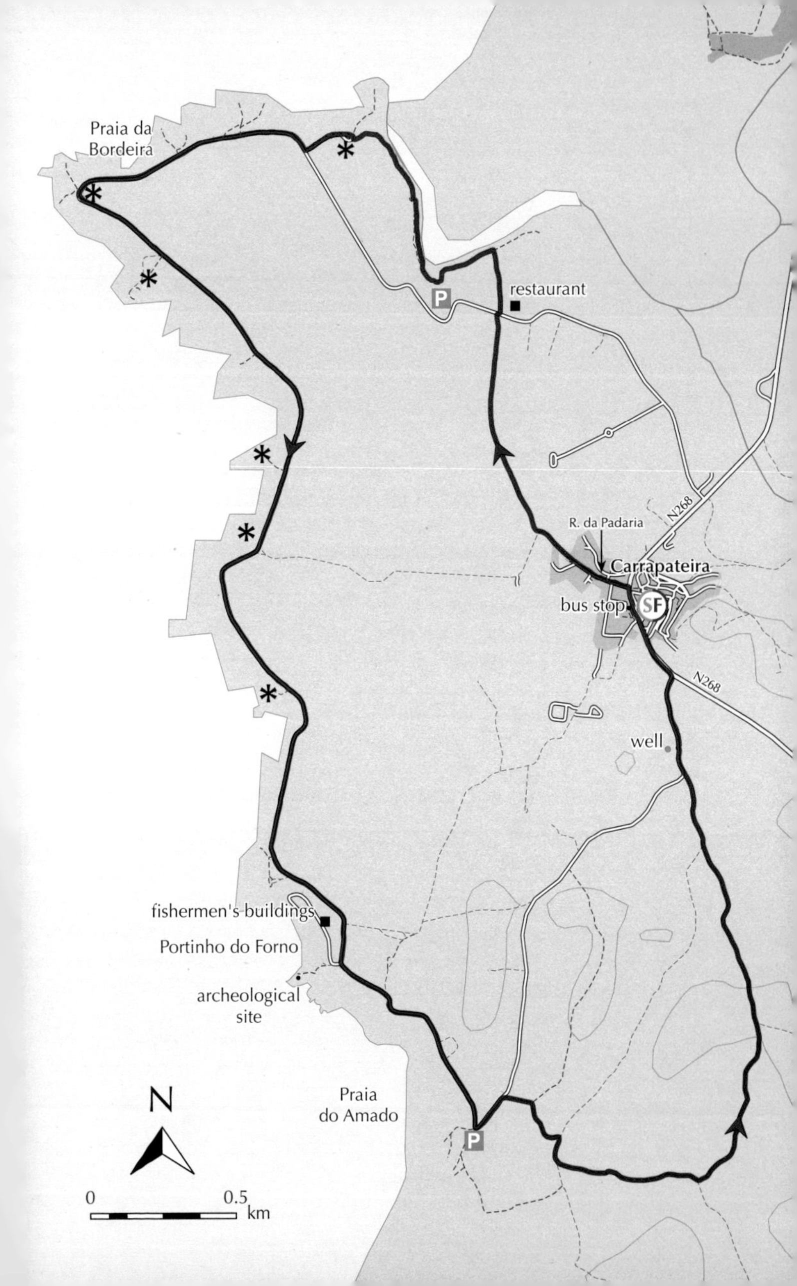
Praia da Bordeira
restaurant
R. da Padaria
Carrapateira
bus stop
SF
N268
N268
well
fishermen's buildings
Portinho do Forno
archeological site
Praia do Amado
N
0
0.5 km

Craggy coastline towards Portinho do Forno

Notice Carrapateira's houses on the left. There is a small port on the right and then walk past the Sitio do Forno restaurant by the road. After the restaurant there is **archaeological site**, an Islamic fishermen's settlement, by the ocean. You can follow the boardwalk to visit it. Continue along the track, passing some buildings and about 12min after the archaeological site, arrive at **Praia do Amado** car park. After the first parking area, keep left on a track as the sign indicates (between two car parks) and a few minutes later leave the track to the right on a dirt track (signposted). Almost immediately, ignore a track on the left and keep right. Then ignore the next track on the left, and keep right as signposted. Before reaching the hills, keep left on a signposted track.

There is a small stream along the track and small, steep hills dominate the views. Ignore the track on the right, and keep left as signposted. Continue slightly uphill on the track, and arrive at a small junction with a ramshackle pen (containing angry dogs when the authors visited).

Keep straight on as the green/blue signs indicate. Carrapateira is in front of you, and there are hills on the right with some small antennas. Ignore the track on the left and head towards the village. About 30min after leaving Praia do Amado, emerge onto a surfaced road and keep right towards the village. Pass a **well** and arrive at a tarmac road at the edge of the village. Keep left and walk back to the village centre, which is a few minutes away.

WALK 31

Bordeira circular

Start/finish	The small church at the centre of Bordeira village (N37.196560, W8.861221)
Distance	6km
Total ascent/descent	80m
Grade	1
Time	1hr 30min
Refreshments	Bar at Bordeira. None along the way
Access	Bordeira is located on the N268 road 19km north of Vila do Bispo. The N268 road can be accessed from the N125. There are plenty of places to park in the small village. Alternatively, there is parking by the road where the trail leaves the tarmac road. There is a bus stop in the village but the bus service is very limited (twice a week) and you have to seek information about buses locally in Lagos or in Portimão! Therefore, this walk might only be accessible by car.

This short, signposted walk is part of the PR2AZJ trail, following the tracks near Bordeira village. Birdsong and whispering trees accompany you on this tranquil trail, and low rolling hills and meadows dominate the views.

▸ From the **church**, walk to the main road (N268) that runs just outside the village. Cross the tarmac road and on its other side, start on the yellow/red-marked dirt track. When the track splits, keep right as the sign indicates; cross the small streambed and carry straight on. At the intersection, keep left. There is some cultivated land with a **small building** on the left hand side. Pass an animal pen, and when the track splits, keep right and slightly uphill on the stony track. Rolling hills dominate the views, and eucalyptus trees grow alongside the track. Ignore a track on the right, and carry straight on as the

The small parish church of Bordeira was built during the 18th century and is only open for mass.

yellow/red sign indicates. Ignore another track on the left and continue straight on. Views open up to rolling hills as you descend.

Notice some cork oaks by the track. Ignore another track on the left, carry straight on and cross a streambed (there are stepping stones if the water is too high). Follow the track and a few minutes later cross a shallow streambed again. It might not be obvious in dry season. Arrive at a junction, go left on the wide track and soon notice some beehives on the right-hand side. Low, pointy hills dominate the landscape and there is a *nora* (old well of Moorish construction) hidden among the bushes a bit further from the track on the left. Keep on the well-trodden track, ignoring a track on the right. Mediterranean pines, like small umbrellas, stand on the hillside.

The way of the stream – which can be recognized in the shrubs – is almost parallel to the track. Walk slightly uphill and about 50min after starting from

The 18th century church of Bordeira

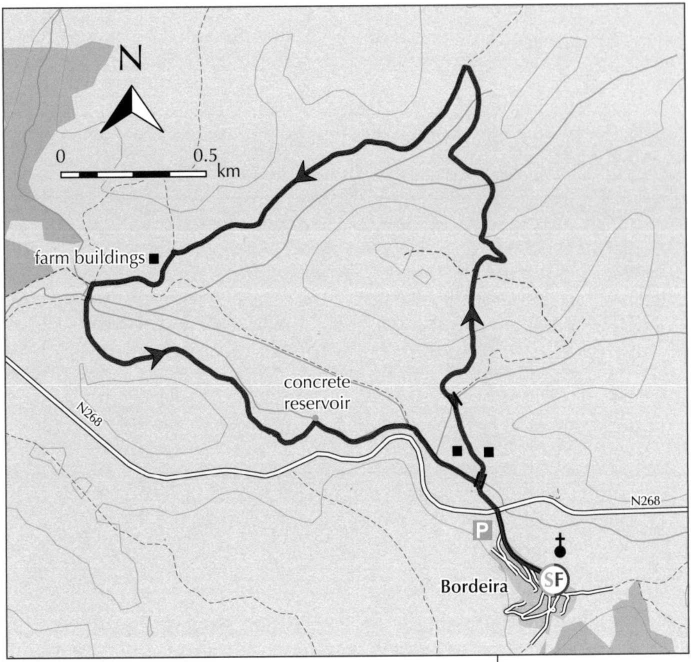

Bordeira, arrive at a signposted junction. Turn left as the 'Bordalete 50m, Bordeira 2.5km' sign indicates and pass some disused **farm buildings**. Skirt around the buildings and arrive at another junction. Go left towards Bordeira, 2km. Cross the streambed on a concrete bridge and keep left as signposted.

Follow this track snaking alongside low hills (you can see the disused farm buildings on the left and soon they are behind you). A meadow, bounded by hills, stretches out on your left. ▸ When the track splits, keep left as the sign indicates. Pass a small (possibly dry) **concrete reservoir**. The stream runs alongside the track and there is some cultivated land on the right. At the junction, go right and reach the asphalt road. Bordeira is on its other side.

Young eucalyptus trees, like thin matchsticks, cling to the slopes of low hills. Cork oaks grow by the track.

WALK 32

Fortaleza da Arrifana circular

Start/finish	Fortaleza da Arrifana near Arrifana Beach (N37.296412, W8.873252)
Distance	10.5km
Total ascent/descent	200m
Grade	2
Time	3hr
Refreshments	Restaurants, bars at Praia da Arrifana, and there is a restaurant at the car park by the fort. Take plenty of water for the walk.
Access	The fort is located on the cliffs at the end of the M1003–1 road 10km west of Aljezur. The M1003–1 road is accessible from the N120 road. There are plenty of places to park by the fort.

Follow the undulating coastal path from the fort to the remains of Ribat da Arrifa. The scenery is dominated by the dramatic coastline. After the remains of Ribat da Arrifa, for a short section you walk between the houses of Vale da Telha and then follow some sandy paths back to the fort.

Arrifana Fort was built in 1635 to help to protect the fishing industry in the area. It was damaged by the 1755 earthquake; restoration works were carried out in 1762 and in 1771 but the fort was abandoned by the 19th century.

Start on the tarmac road with the fort behind you. The trail starts on the left, just after the building. The ocean and the fort will be on your left. The houses of Arrifana are on the right and you can see the silhouette of Fóia in the distance. As you follow the narrow path steeply downhill, the landscape is dominated by dark rocks. A ravine with a stream stretches inland. There are three small paths, but take the path on the right towards the ravine.

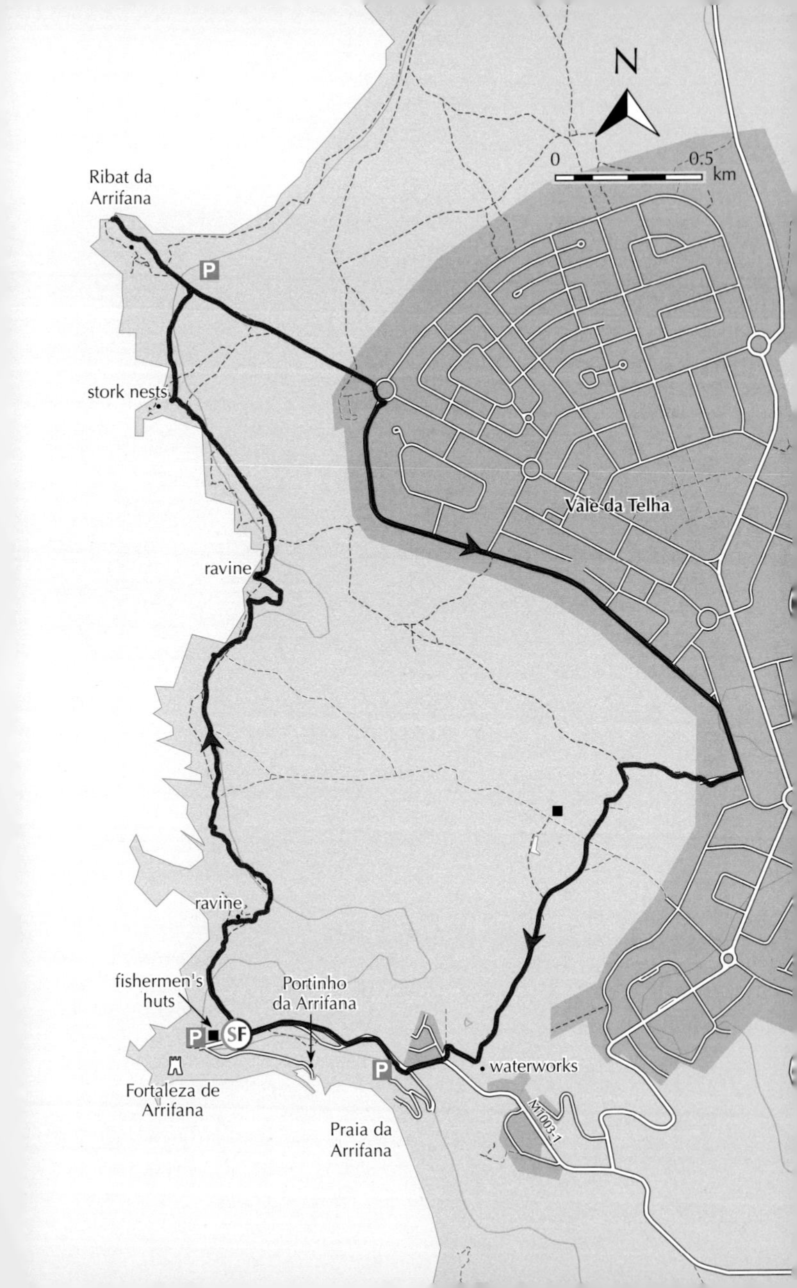

N
0
0.5
km
Ribat da Arrifana
P
stork nests
Vale da Telha
ravine
ravine
fishermen's huts
Portinho da Arrifana
P
SF
P
waterworks
M1003-1
Fortaleza de Arrifana
Praia da Arrifana

The dramatic coast near Arrifana Fort

About 15–20min from the fort descend to the first **ravine**, cross the stream over some rocks, and continue uphill on the slightly overgrown path. You can see the stream joins the ocean on the left. Ascend on the shrub-covered hill with views towards Vale da Telha on the right.

Walk towards the ocean on the edge, and on reaching the cliff keep right, with the ocean on your left. Continue slightly uphill and then descend to another ravine. Cross the ravine and continue uphill, with some views to an outcrop and a small stony beach. Ignore a dirt track on the right, and stay on a narrow path closer to the cliffs. ◄ You can also enjoy some great views of the coastline and shrub-covered hills. Another dirt track

Like a mysterious skeleton, there are sharp rocks sticking out of the ocean floor.

joins from the right, but carry straight on alongside the ocean. Descend to a tiny ravine with a small stream, and then continue uphill on its other side. There are views to a small black rock-bordered bay. Notice a dirt track on the right, but continue along the path.

Follow the contour of the coastline, and you can see a group of houses in the distance. Soon turning away from the ocean, descend steeply to a ravine and head back towards the ocean on the overgrown path. You might hear trickling water. Cross a ravine with a small stream and continue uphill on a huge flat rock, on the other side of the ravine. You might see other paths in the area, but try to stay close to the ocean. The green/blue signposted trail joins from the right, but continue straight on, on the sandy path, which is marked with green/blue signs on this section. There is a black rock-bordered bay on the left, and looking back you can even see the fort in the distance. Continue along the shrub-lined sandy path. You might spot **storks nesting** on the dark rocks on the left. ▶

The Vicentina coast in the Algarve is the only place in Europe where storks nest on sea cliffs.

Follow the green/blue signs, and keep left as the sign indicates. In the springtime small flowers add a dash of purple, yellow, pink and white to the green shrubs and yellowish sand.

There is a dirt track on the right, and the ruins of **Ribat da Arrifana** on the left. Arrive at the parking area and ruins about 1hr 30min after leaving the Forteleza da Arrifana. The trail continues on the dirt track towards the village from the parking area, but first head to the outcrop for great views. You can admire a blackish sea stack only accessible to birds.

The ruins of **Ribat da Arrifana** were only discovered in 2002. It was founded by Ibn Qasi around 1130 and abandoned in 1151. It was part of a bigger metropolis. Every year for a few months an excavation takes place, but the rest of the time the area is mainly covered up. Some ruins can be seen but there are no information boards or signs in the area. In 2013 it was classified as a Portuguese National Monument.

Looking back towards the fort

The green/blue marked trail continues along the cliff; however from the car park area near the ruins, follow the dirt track inland towards the houses. A few minutes later – by the first house – the dirt track becomes a tarmac road. From the huge roundabout, go right and continue between neat villas. Ignore any roads joining from the left and carry straight on. About 20min after arriving at the village, at the junction keep right, and then go right again on the first available road. It is a 200m dead end street and just before reaching the house at the end of the road, go right on a small path. Continue towards a ramshackle building. When the path splits, keep left (with the ramshackle building on your right) and follow the green/blue signs on the sandy path. Cross a stream. ◂

You can see Vale da Telha's houses on the left.

Keep left when the sign indicates, as the other path goes towards the ramshackle building in front of you. Follow the wide path with ramshackle building on the right. At the junction, continue straight on with ruins on the right. When another track joins from the left, keep right towards the ocean as the sign indicates. Notice a small reservoir on the right.

Descend to a small stream and cross over on some rocks. Arrive by a small, fenced **waterworks** about 25–30min after leaving the village on the path. Go uphill on the tarmac road towards the houses. Keep left and arrive at a tarmac road junction. Continue straight through **Praia da Arrifana** and carry on downhill for 900m, and arrive at the fort.

WALK 33

Praia da Amoreira circular

Start/finish	Praia da Amoreira car park (N37.352257, W8.843625)
Distance	7km
Total ascent/descent	85m
Grade	1
Time	2hr
Refreshments	Snack bar at Praia da Amoreira, none along the trail.
Access	From Aljezur take the N120 road then about 900m after leaving the town, turn left as the Amoreira sign indicates. And then follow this winding surfaced road for 7km to the beach.

This, short waymarked trail starts from a beach then for a short section it joins the GR11 long-distance trail and then follows some dirt tracks. Information boards – about the wildlife and plants in the area – are located along the first section of the trail.

From the **car park**, facing the ocean and the restaurant building, start ascending on the sandy path on the right. There are several information boards located along the first section of the trail. When the path splits, keep left, and stay closer to the ocean for further fine views. ▶ Keep on the well-trodden path as the green/blue sign indicates. About 30min after starting from the car park, the path turns away from the coast and runs through a small pine forest. At the junction, carry straight on as the sign indicates and soon pass a **house**. Ignore a track on the left, and carry straight on. After the woods, walk across an open area and at the dirt track junction, continue straight on. The silhouette of Fóia is noticeable in the distance.

The craggy coast stretches into the distance.

Ignore a track on the right and keep slightly left towards a building. There is a crumbling wall and a disused building by the track. Pass a **house** (right side of the

Well-trodden path along the coast

track) and when the track splits, take the right branch as the sign indicates (the other path goes towards a ramshackle building).

Emerge onto a dirt track about 30min after leaving the woods. Keep right as the 'GR11 E9 Aljezur' sign indicates. Shrubs populate the area alongside the dirt track, and you have views towards the sandy beach and some houses in the distance. Ignore the track on the left and continue to the right as the white/red sign indicates. When the track splits, keep left. Follow the dirt track, and at the next junction go right. From here the trail is marked again with green/blue signs. Almost immediately, at the next junction, keep right. As you descend, notice the small ravine on your left, and some eucalyptus trees alongside the track. Soon a building with a crumbling roof comes into view.

Keep left near the **ruins of a building**. Soon notice another ruin near the track and head towards a car park. Emerge onto a tarmac road near the parking area, keep right and a few minutes later arrive back at Praia Amoreira car park.

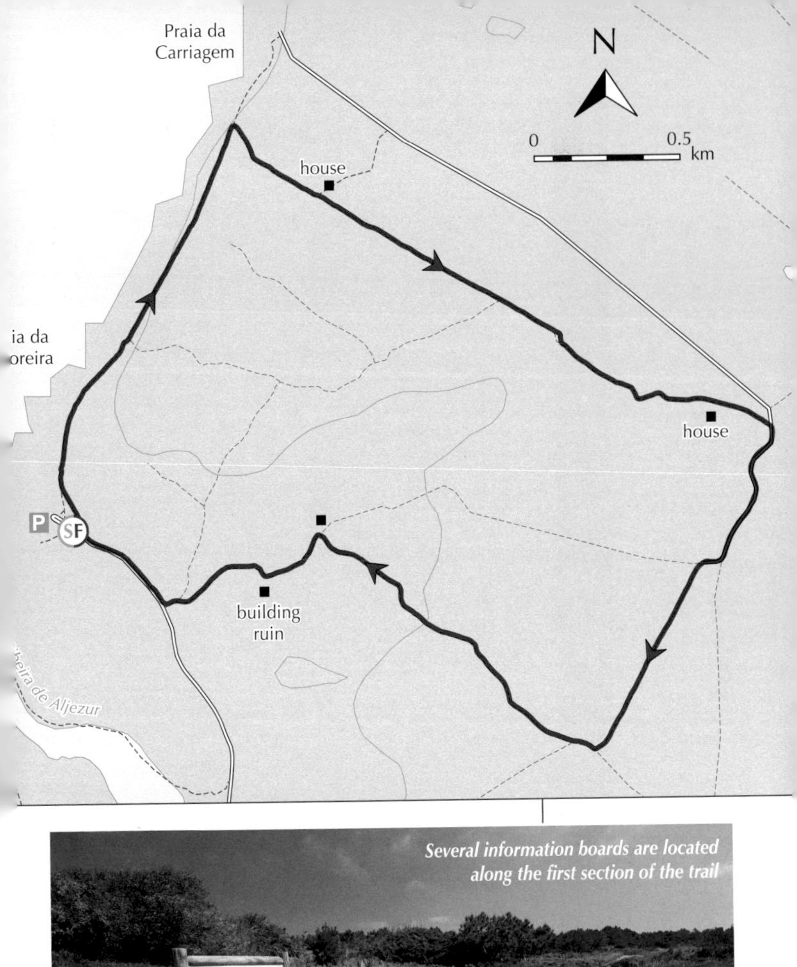

Several information boards are located along the first section of the trail

APPENDIX A

Route summary table

Walk	Start/finish	Distance	Total ascent/ descent	Grade	Time	Page
Eastern Algarve						29
1	Furnazinhas	8.5km	185m	2	2hr 30min–3hr	31
2	Furnazinhas	8km	215m	2	2hr 30min	36
3	Mealha	6.5km	155m	1	2hr	40
4	Corte Garcia	6.5km	250m	2	2hr	44
5	1.5km west of Querença	4km	45m	1	1hr 15min	47
6	Penina	7.5km	250m	2	2hr 30min	50
7	Paderne castle	3.5km	50m	1	1hr	55
Central region						59
8	4km west of Silves	6.5km	110m	1	2hr–2hr 15min	61
9	1km west of Odelouca dam	4km	125m	1	1hr 30min	65
10	Monchique	13km	615m	3	3hr 30min–4hr	69
11	Caldas de Monchique/Monchique or Caldas de Monchique	12km	550m/305m	3	4hr	74
12	Fóia	7.5km	305m	2	2hr 30min	80
13	Fóia	13.5km	610m	3	4hr 30min	84

14	Marmelete	9.5km	330m	2	3hr	89
15	Barragem da Bravura	7.5km	160m	1	2hr 15min	**94**
16	Barão de São João	7km	155m	1	2hr	97
17	Barão de São João	10km	275m/275m	2	3hr	**101**
South Coast						**105**
18	Albufeira/Galé	8.5km	130m/145m	2	2hr 30min–3hr	**107**
19	Praia do Vale do Olival/Praia da Marinha	9.5km	145m/135m	2	3hr–3hr 30min	113
20	Praia da Marinha/Praia Vale de Centeanes	7km	180m/170m	2	2hr 30min	**118**
21	Praia Vale de Centeanes/Ferragudo	12km	245m/235m	3	4hr–4hr 30min	123
22	Portimão	4.5km	100m	1	1hr 15min	**129**
23	Alvor	5km	10m	1	1hr 15min	132
24	Lagos/Luz	10km	270m/280m	2	3hr–3hr 30min	**135**
25	Luz/Salema	13km	250m/260m	3	4hr–4hr 30min	141
26	Salema/Sagres	17km	400m/395m	3	5hr 30min–6hr	**146**
27	Sagres/Cabo de São Vicente	10km	255m/225m	2	3hr	153
Vicentina Coast						**159**
28	Cabo de São Vicente	10km	120m	2	2hr 30min–3hr	161
29	2.5km north west of Vila do Bispo	11km	290m	2	3hr–3hr 30min	**165**
30	Carrapateira	12km	165m	2	3hr 30min	169
31	Bordeira	6km	80m	1	1hr 30min	**173**
32	Fortaleza de Arrifana	10.5km	200m	2	3hr	176
33	Praia da Amoreira	7km	85m	1	2hr	**181**

APPENDIX B

Portuguese-English glossary

On the trails

Portuguese	English
albufeira	lagoon or reservoir
água	water
área de piquenique	picnic area
barragem	dam
barranco	ravine
caminho	path
cascata	waterfall
castelo	castle
cerro	hill
convento	convent
farol	lighthouse
fonte	fountain/spring
forte	fort
fortaleza	fortress
ilha	island
jardin	garden
levada	irrigation channel
lago	lake
mina(s)	mine(s)
monte	hill, mountain
miradouro	viewpoint
parque	park
parque nacional	national/natural park or reserve
percurso	route
percurso pedestre	pedestrian route
pico	peak
planalto	plateau

ponte	bridge
praia	beach
privado	private
ribeiro	stream
rio	river
rocha	rock
serra	mountain range
trilha	trail
vale	valley
via	route/way

In town

Portuguese	English
casa	house
estação de onibus	bus station
estação ferroviária	train station
estrada	road
farmácia	pharmacy
igreja	church
paragem	bus stop
rua	street

Warnings and emergencies

Portuguese	English
atenção	attention
bombeiros	fire service
emergência	emergency
perigo	danger

APPENDIX C

Useful contacts

Tourist information

Tourist offices

Albufeira Tourist Office
Rua 5 de Outubro
8200–109 Albufeira
tel +351 289 585 279

Carvoeiro Tourist Office
Largo da Praia
8400–517 Carvoeiro LGA
tel +351 282 357 728

Faro Tourist Office
Rua da Misericórdia,
8–118000–269 Faro
tel +351 289 803 604

Lagos Tourist Office
Praça Gil Eanes
(Antigos Paços do Concelho)
8600–668 Lagos
tel +351 282 763 031

Monchique Tourist Office
Largo S. Sebastião
8550–0000 Monchique
tel +351 282 911 189

Portimão Tourist Office
Largo 1 Dezembro,
8500–538 Portimão
tel +351 282 402 487

Sagres Tourist Office
Rua Comandante Matoso
8650–357 Sagres
tel +351 282 624 873

Websites

Visit Portugal
www.visitportugal.com

Visit Algarve
www.visitalgarve.pt

Walks in Portugal
www.wiportugal.org

Natural Pt
(a project to support the biodiversity, economy, heritage and identity of Portugal's natural spaces)
www.natural.pt/en

Portugal Visitor
(tourism guide)
www.portugalvisitor.com

Portugal Resident
(news website in English that includes restaurant and events listings)
www.portugalresident.com

Transport

Flights

Faro airport
www.faro-airport.com

Flights from the UK

Air Portugal
www.flytap.com

British Airways
www.britishairways.com

Easyjet
www.easyjet.com

Jet2
www.Jet2.com

Ryanair
www.ryanair.com

Price comparison sites
www.kayak.co.uk
www.skyscanner.net

Buses

Algarve Bus
(unofficial but informative and up-to-date bus timetable)
www.algarvebus.info

Eva Transportes
www.eva-bus.com

Frota Azul Algarve
www.frotazul-algarve.pt

A Onda
(urban buses around Lagos)
www.aonda.pt

Car rental

Major car hire companies are present such as Avis, Budget, Europcar, Hertz, Goldcar, Sixt as well as Centauro. You can compare the deals on:

www.autoeurope.co.uk

www.holidayautos.com

www.kayak.co.uk

www.rentalcars.com

www.travelsupermarket.com

Accommodation

www.airbnb.co.uk

www.booking.com

www.expedia.com

www.trivago.co.uk

Camping

www.en.camping.info/portugal/algarve/campsites

Emergencies

European emergency number
112

Fire emergency
117

DOWNLOAD THE ROUTES IN GPX FORMAT

All the routes in this guide are available for download from:

www.cicerone.co.uk/994/GPX

as GPX files. You should be able to load them into most formats of mobile device, whether GPS or smartphone.

When you go to this link, you will be asked for your email address and where you purchased the guide, and have the option to subscribe to the Cicerone e-newsletter.